Make to Know: From Spaces of Uncertai[nty]

: about creativity. The book upends popular [notions]

ad the event of discovery that happens throug[h]

chelangelo, who "saw th[e] ~~in the stone, ##~~ artis[t]

out knowing their work as ~~the~~

creative journey itself." As Duchman wea[ves]

re learn about writers of all stripes as they [c]

t visual artists and what they understand fr[om]

cts and the iterative *process* ~~way~~ of solving problem[s]

provisational performan[ce]. Make to Know is

and, in the end, a [stet] will have significant im[pact]

f Uncertainty to Creative Discovery will

~~opular~~ notions of innate artistic and visionary *[italic]*

hrough the act of making. ○ In contrast to the

~~t o,"~~ one, the artists and designers Buchman in[?]

age in the doing. Make to Know explores Th[?]

~~man~~ *[ital]* weaves together the vivid stories of his n[?]

nusicians facing the surprises ~~musicians fa[cing]~~

Buchman weaves together the vivid stories

italic *Discovery* will change the way you

nate artistic and visionary genius and probes

f making. In contrast to the classic tale of

ners Buchman interviews for this book talk

ke to Know explores the revelatory nature of

r the vivid stories of his multiple conversatio

ive spaces of uncertainty "the blank page";

rials they encounter; about designers and ar

t actors and musicians facing the surprises o

will, ultimately, open a road to your own ma

for how you live. Make to Know: From Spa

ray you think about creativity. The book upe.

robes instead the event of discovery that happ

of Michelangelo, who "saw the angel in

is book talk about knowing their work as the

g nature of the creative journey itself. As

rsations, we learn about writers of all actors

MAKE TO KNOW

Lorne M. Buchman

MAKE TO KNOW

From Spaces of Uncertainty
to Creative Discovery

38 illustrations

For Ruchul

First published in the United Kingdom in 2021 by
Thames & Hudson Ltd, 181A High Holborn, London WC1V 7QX

First published in the United States of America in 2021 by
Thames & Hudson Inc., 500 Fifth Avenue, New York, New York 10110

Make to Know: From Spaces of Uncertainty to Creative Discovery
© 2021 Thames & Hudson Ltd

Text © 2021 Lorne M. Buchman

Edited by Camilla Rockwood
Typeset by Mark Bracey

British Library Cataloguing-in-Publication Data
A catalogue record for this book is available from the British Library

Library of Congress Control Number 2021934208

ISBN 978-0-500-02452-2

Printed and bound in Slovenia by DZS-Grafik d.o.o.

Be the first to know about our new releases,
exclusive content and author events by visiting
thamesandhudson.com
thamesandhudsonusa.com
thamesandhudson.com.au

CONTENTS

Chapter 6

IMPLICATIONS FOR HOW WE LIVE — 182

CREATIVE UNCERTAINTY: THE MAKING OF THE APPLE STORE

The true is precisely what is made.
—GIAMBATTISTA VICO[1]

To ask for the whole thing cut and dried at once is a great error. There is no use sitting down waiting for clarity, believing that your work will reveal itself in a flash and show you the road to it free of charge. You have to grope your way in good faith...
—VILHELM EKELUND[2]

One morning in the fall of 1999, the phone rang at the San Francisco office of design firm Eight Inc. On the other end was Andrea Nordemann, longtime assistant to Steve Jobs. Tim Kobe, CEO of the firm, took the call. He and his partners had worked with Apple on the product launch of its colored iMacs a year earlier and, more recently, Kobe had sent Jobs his ideas for creating a signature retail outlet.

"Hey," Nordemann began, "Steve is interested in that retail stuff. He would like to see your retail credentials."

By "retail stuff," Nordemann was referring to what would eventually become the Apple Store, a groundbreaking facility that is now a clear and unmistakable articulation of Apple's brand. At that time, however, the process of how it would be created was anything but clear—at least from the perspective of Kobe, its lead designer. To hear Kobe's narrative is to learn, with some surprise, that the Apple Store came about through a process riddled with failure and unpredictable turns.

"Okay, that would be great," Kobe told Nordemann. "We can show him our credentials."

"Well," she said, "he's in the car, and he'll be there in fifteen minutes." The unexpected turns of the process were already under way.

Kobe recalls the importance of his firm's relationship with Jobs even before that call. "The creation of the Apple Store really began with our relationship in 1998, getting to a point where Steve trusted us, our opinion. When Steve saw the colored iMacs, he realized he had something that was no longer an appliance, but a consumer product that was a colorful and beautiful thing. We just put them all on a big light table at the MacWorld trade show, illuminated them, and let the stunning qualities of the product come through."

Apple changed the game with the colored iMac. "It was unheard of in that industry prior to that. Beige, beige, and gray. Nothing else." Kobe and his team leveraged the moment of Apple's revolutionary turn to color, and their work pleased Jobs no end. "He recognized we weren't about making shapes for the trade shows. It was, instead, about making the product the hero. He thought we really got it."

During that period in the late 1990s, however, Kobe actually had his eye on a much bigger idea: a retail facility for Apple. "We were doing three or four events a year. The first [color iMac] launch was at MacWorld in San Francisco—and then New York, Paris, and Tokyo. But even before we were doing those shows, I wrote a white paper for Steve explaining why Apple should create its own retail program. We had just finished working with Nike and North Face, both manufacturers whose products were being sold by third-party retailers. Nike, for example, was being sold at Foot Locker, but in that context the brand couldn't stand out. Nike couldn't sufficiently communicate what they were about, their values. And so they started the Niketown program to sell their entire product line, but they had to do it strategically, without sacrificing the sales volume of their dealers, like Foot Locker. It made perfect sense to me that Apple needed to do something similar with flagship stores."

Kobe's instincts were spot on, because it turned out that Jobs was keenly interested in finding a way to increase control of Apple's message and brand. The moment was ripe for a flagship idea. The reality of Apple products sitting on shelves next to various Microsoft and PC offerings, together with salespeople who lacked deep knowledge of Apple products, was for Jobs a serious concern. Eight Inc. had also worked with Apple on designing a "shop-in-shop" idea that they had tested in multiple locations in Japan. According to Kobe's partner, Wilhelm Oehl, the shop-in-shop experiment was the prelude to the Apple Store, a live prototype that opened up possibilities.[3] The Japan pilot continued in the United States (primarily through CompUSA in both San Francisco and New York), producing increased sales but not fully solving the problems of third-party retail and the central objectives of a brand that wanted greater control of its message and identity.

Enter Tim Kobe and his white paper, "Flagship Retail Feasibility Report," originally drafted in 1996. He defined the opportunity in the Executive Summary, and planted the seed for an ambitious retail project.

> The image of Apple Computer in a consistent, controlled distribution of the Apple Message is critical to successful renewal strategy. Apple product information and image at the retail level has been confusing at best. The industry, as well as the general media, have seemed to define the Company more than the Company itself. Confusion during the transition at Apple is natural but there is distinct lack of "information tools" available for Apple. With the industry growing more competitive, trade show formats are not enough. Serious consideration must be given to additional formats if Apple is to successfully implement its strategic renewal.[4]

Fifteen minutes after Nordemann's call, Jobs arrived at Eight Inc. and asked to meet in the conference room. But the firm, at the time, didn't have one. "We had a table, and that was it. My partner Wilhelm

Oehl and I sat down with him and began. In those days, you still presented your work on transparencies. We had 4×5 transparencies of photographs of things we had done. We showed him the work we did for Nike. We showed him the work with North Face. And some other stuff too. He takes it all in, looks at us, and says, 'What would you say if I told you I didn't like any of this work, and that none of it looks like Apple?' Wilhelm's jaw fell on the table."

Kobe steeled himself, looked Jobs in the eye, and spoke candidly. "'We designed this work for Nike and this work for North Face.' 'Fine,' Steve says, 'but why should I hire you if none of this looks like Apple?' And I said, 'The reason you should hire us is because none of this looks like Apple—and we will do for Apple what is right for Apple.' He paused for a long time, knowing I had done the old reversal on him. I knew Steve had employed that tactic to give us a hard push. He wanted to see if we would stand up or fall. Anyway, he got up and walked over to the door, shook our hands, and said, 'I don't know if you guys have enough retail yet.' And then he walked out. Wilhelm and I looked at each other—does that mean we are hired or not? Two days later, he called and said 'Come on down, let's start working.' We started on the whiteboard."

We started on the whiteboard? How could that be? The deeply imaginative Steve Jobs would certainly have had a vision for this revolutionary retail outlet. He must have known what he wanted. After all, most of us recognize him, deservedly, as the genius and architect of Apple and its innovative products. Surely that beautiful store, existing today in thousands of locations and always crowded, was a product of the vision of its celebrated leader. The wide open spaces, the community display tables, the Genius Bar, the invitation to engage with products by virtue of their presentation alone, the choice materials and fixtures strategically deployed, the glass and the wood, the precise use of color, the intuitive layout of the whole—all of it, one would think, must have sprung, like Zeus birthing Athena, from the head of Jobs. But is that how it came about? We know the Apple Store transformed the retail landscape at the turn of the 21st century in the United States and abroad. What was the actual process that led to this remarkable outcome?

As Kobe explains during our interview for this book, there was, in fact, absolutely no driving vision for the design of the store. Not even close. He believes that Steve Jobs was a man who made decisions through an iterative process and, in the end, through a reliance on intuition. "Steve was very quick at running through a logic tree and saying, 'If this, then this—and here's a bust in your logic, go back and work on it.' But if you made it through the logic tree, then he would flip over the other side, which is very intuitive, and let you know if it didn't feel right."

"It sounds like he was, in certain ways, a guy who needed to engage creatively to know what he wanted," I suggest. "Stories abound that Steve Jobs had to dive into things, construct them, feel them, until he knew what the result should be."

"Absolutely," Kobe confirms. "We started with bubble diagrams for the store, just saying 'let's try this or look at that.' We then went from sketches and drawings to small physical models. We were making a physical model each week of different things. And then we went to full-size models in a mock-up room. We produced some component of the store every week in foam-core mock-ups. Steve would walk around the models and look at them, fully realized in space. It all evolved until we found what felt like Apple. Along the way, we found a lot that didn't work, that was too self-conscious, too technical, etc. When it didn't work, we would just tear the models down, or move them around, rebuild them, adjust things.

"Steve didn't even have an idea actually about how big a store he wanted," he continues. "At one point, he said he wanted it to be big, and we said, 'Okay, but you just scaled everything down to four products, you know, the PowerMac, iMac, iBook, and PowerBook. If you want a big store we have to put stuff in it.' That's how basic it was. In the end, we were guided by the need to express what Apple's core values were about. That's where all the different design elements of the retail space eventually developed."[5]

There was certainly a business idea behind the store, but it was an idea that had already been in play with a number of companies and brands at the time (North Face, Nike, Sony, Disney, Levi's, and several others). What ultimately made the design of the Apple stores

Above and below: Exterior and interior of the first Apple Store that opened on May 19, 2001, at Tysons Corner Center mall in Virginia.

distinctive (and distinguished) was the way in which the design team, as Kobe explains above, *led with key values*; the driving principles of Apple mobilized them. Those principles together served as the entry point into a project filled with uncertainty, igniting a making process that carried forward into the design. "When you think about what made Apple special," Kobe reflects, "it was about technology accessible to people other than engineers. That's what the mouse did—it wasn't keystrokes and backstrokes and writing code. It was about making technology human—that was Apple's core differentiation, their core value proposition. Steve fought hard for the Macintosh (and was beat up about it) because he knew that was the right thing for technology if you ever wanted it to find mass adoption."

Today, with hindsight, we can see the multiple ways in which Eight Inc. manifested these Apple values in their design. As Kobe tells it: "You had to have a store that was easy to use. It meant making everything comfortable and inviting. In contrast to, say, traditional apparel retail, which is very dense, the Apple Store is very open, intuitive—like the products themselves—and we were trying to present those qualities through a variety of touchpoints. That meant detailed attention to the physical things, the environment, and the people attending to the consumer. Steve wanted people working at the store who knew just enough about technology but were not so absorbed that the human element was missing. He wanted a balance of the engaging, warm individual who also had technological knowhow."

The collaborating team grew to involve key participants including Millard (Mickey) Drexler, then CEO of Gap Inc., whom Jobs recruited to Apple's board of directors in 1999. Drexler was a celebrated retail expert at the time and contributed significantly to the conversation. Kobe explains: "He was of the school of a very dense retail product, heavy—'stack it high, watch it fly'—the old retail. Steve discovered that he didn't like that. He wanted it to be the opposite of that experience."

But the open, airy feel of the final design might not have evolved in the same way without Drexler's provocations. According to Walter Isaacson's biography, *Steve Jobs*, and similarly noted in a case study produced by the business school INSEAD, Drexler was the one who suggested that the design team develop "a full-scale prototype in a warehouse near the firm's headquarters in Cupertino...down to the smallest details."[6] This idea was apparently kept secret from the public, and Kobe tells me at length about how the space was used to explore ideas and test concepts. In this context, according to Kobe, Jobs' appreciation of the iterative process of making became glaringly evident. Jobs himself has also been quoted as celebrating this full-scale arena of test and discovery: "One of the best pieces of advice Mickey gave us was to rent a warehouse and build a prototype store."[7]

Kobe recognized the importance of collaboration in improvising the design. A group would converge weekly at these "Tuesday meetings." "We probably had fifteen people in that meeting every week, engaged in the evolution and the making process. A lot changed along the way."

I ask Kobe to cite specifics. For example, how did they find their way to the design feature of those tables to display product? "We were experimenting with different fixtures. We were doing one a week, and it got to the point where the design started to be too self-conscious." And so they went back to basics. "We needed something that supported the idea that the product was the hero. And if the product was the hero, then the design display needed to take a second position to that. We also realized that we couldn't change the store every time the product changed. Steve was clearly going to be developing new products. So we created this natural landscape—large wood tables. They were like these big Parsons tables."

He continues, "And we would meet every week, build models, build full-size prototypes, and we ultimately got to where we were arguing over eighth-inch increments of the thickness of the table. But the whole process, the *making*, was a search for what felt right and what matched Apple's values. The tables needed to be generous, spacious."

"Did you know," I ask, "the effect it would have in creating a sense of community energy around the table, something that I think is a brilliant stroke of that retail environment?"

"It all goes back to the making process," he says. "You have to experience it, feel it, to know. That's what we did. Happy accidents, I suppose."

Another discovery of the design journey had to do with the lighting in the store and how it influenced the look of the products. Working with a lighting designer based in Florida, the team discovered a thorny problem that they needed to solve—a problem identified through the reality of elements in relationship in physical space.

"Apple does amazing product photography," Kobe says. "When you look at that product photography you see beautiful highlights—everything comes from the soft box lighting effect and it's what makes the product look good. What we discovered was when we placed a poster over the tables, the product didn't look as good as the photograph above it. We were unintentionally sending a bad message; we were, in effect, telling people they shouldn't trust Apple—that we say one thing and do another. The product has to be just as spectacular when you see it live."

The challenge, in Kobe's words, was for him and his collaborators to find a way to "look at the product on the wall and the product on the table—and see it as equally beautiful. There is integrity to it all." Again, they experimented with all kinds of ideas. "We spent a long time at it and eventually started working with a product called Nomad. It was a vinyl heat-formed material. We kept doing mock-ups and more mock-ups, trying to get to where we had just the right amount of soft box light as well as some color highlights and other accidents. We got there and the product looked as beautiful as the image."[8]

Designing the store had everything to do with understanding the experience of the consumer. That driving sense of empathy, however, was not a quality Jobs could simply manifest from a preconceived vision. Together with the team, he had to experiment, explore possibilities, accept some ideas, reject others, iterate, sketch, build models, test material. In short, the store wasn't so much a product of his vision as it was something made, constructed, fashioned in the course of a creative journey. Kobe insists that the making process itself was the way to know that central experience of the customer and the design that would honor it. "Steve put himself in the position of the user. If ideas we presented didn't have the qualities that attracted him, we wouldn't do it. But he wouldn't have known without the process itself."

Kobe offers a final example of the process in a brief anecdote about the design of the Chicago store and its use of stone. "It was Indiana limestone. We had just done a project for Gucci, so I knew exactly what stone was required for Michigan Avenue. We got hold of some Indiana limestone very quickly and then wrestled with how we might treat it. Should it be smooth? Should it be textured? It needed to work in cold weather and snow and ice. I remember we went for two or three months looking at stone samples at different size and scale. Steve was looking at all of this one day and suddenly says, 'You know, we are so stupid. We are doing this all wrong. It rains in Chicago. We are looking at the stone out here in dry, sunny, happy California.' He asked us to go get water and suddenly everybody scrambled to go get buckets of water. And we start throwing the water on the mock-up. We must've spent five hours looking at wet rock and looking at different ways of treating the stone. That informed the rest of the process, and we made sure that the store would look beautiful wet or dry."

Kobe's account of the design of the Apple Store gives evidence of a tremendously successful project that evolved through a creative course of iteration, experimentation, and improvisation. In what is nothing short of a tribute to the powers of progressive ideation, his tale upends any myths about the visionary genius that brought the facility to life. Indeed, Kobe and his collaborators, together with Jobs, leveraged the fundamentals of an applied making that brought them to knowing the design—sketching, prototyping, modeling, problem-solving, testing, research, generating questions that beget questions, happy accidents, multiple dialogues among designers and fellow collaborators.

The story of how the Apple Store was created contains many elements of an experience I call "make to know": the animating concept of this book and one that receives surprisingly little acknowledgement in the wider literature on creativity. It is a process of moving from uncertainty to invention through the very act of making. My ultimate purpose here is to lay bare, through the stories of a diverse and talented group of artists and designers, the revelatory nature of the creative journey itself.

Chapter 1

FRAMING THE QUESTION

We do not know until the shell breaks what kind
of egg we have been sitting on.
—T.S. ELIOT[1]

Had I been blessed with even limited access to my own
mind there would have been no reason to write.
—JOAN DIDION[2]

"I think best in wire," the sculptor Alexander Calder said. In a curious echo, the novelist Umberto Eco confessed in *Postscript to The Name of the Rose*: "When I put Jorge in the library, I did not yet know he was the murderer. He acted on his own...."[3]

The artist Ann Hamilton, talking to me about uncertainty as a creative space for invention, poses a number of penetrating questions in a similar vein. "How do you cultivate a space where you can allow yourself to do something you don't understand at all? How do you cultivate a process that allows you to be responsive to what making might bring? How do you cultivate a space that allows you to dwell in *not knowing*?"

What interests me about the reflections of these three artists is the connection they make between creative engagement and discovery, between making and knowing. For Calder, the idea is evident in his work with wire—in the physical act of manipulating the material of his own creative practice, Calder is *thinking*. He thinks because he makes. For Eco, the writing of the book itself reveals a crucial element of his plot. He knows because he writes. And for Hamilton, she captures her work by cultivating first a space of "not knowing" and a process of invention that emerges through the making itself. She discovers because she creates.

In my own professional life as a theater director, writer, teacher, and college president, I have repeatedly observed that the making of the thing—the play, the book, the classroom experience, the school—is fundamental to the way I learn and know. As a director, I have always marveled at those who could stage a play at their desk, energetically writing notes in the margins of a text. I've never been able to do that. But when I entered a rehearsal hall, working with real actors moving in real space, I could see exactly how I wanted to stage the piece; or, at the very least, I could recognize a clear path from experimentation to realized performance. I needed to "make" in rehearsal before I could "know" a play in execution.

As a writer, I am fascinated by the idea that some books seem to "write themselves." Novelists, in particular, often say things like "The characters told me what they wanted to say." I understand what they mean—I certainly labor much of the time in my writing, but I have also had that exquisite experience of feeling that something else is taking over, that I'm channeling the content of the written work in the optimal state of "flow" so brilliantly elucidated by the psychologist Mihály Csíkszentmihályi. The writing process itself has at times been a revelation, giving me access, as Joan Didion reflects, to something of myself that would otherwise have remained obscure.

A similar make-to-know practice applies in my work as a teacher and as a college president. In those contexts I might have a framework, a generative question, a point of view, and deeply held principles guiding me; but I cannot fully know where I am going until I am engaged in a process and in a realized space of discovery. I need to do the making, engage in the creative act itself, to get to a place of knowing both the work and the ideas behind it.

"Instead of thinking about what to build," designer Tim Brown observes, we should be "building in order to think."[4] Conventional wisdom about creative engagement suggests the opposite sequence:

that the artist envisions first, then manifests that vision in the work created. Many of us have been taught that Michelangelo saw an angel within a block of stone and carved away until he set it free. Some artists I have interviewed confirm that on occasion their work does progress from vision to execution. As the illustrator and artist Esther Pearl Watson puts it: "Sometimes I just know what I want to do; I have the vision, and I make it happen"—although she adds that this is a rare occurrence.

But the majority of makers I have interviewed for this book do not see their work as the product of predetermined vision. Instead, they recognize that what they produce evolves from the process of making itself. Their observations expose a nuanced and multifaceted sense of creative engagement and its power to surprise. These are artists and designers who talk about how they *make to know*. This is a book of stories of writers filling blank sheets of paper, designers solving complex problems, installation artists engaging space and materials, and musicians and actors improvising composition and performance. It explores how artists talk about what the creative process itself might reveal.

"The truth is," *Calvin and Hobbes* cartoonist Bill Watterson has observed, "most of us discover where we are headed when we arrive."[5]

FAMILIAR AND UNRECOGNIZED

Everyone to whom I have spoken, whether formally or informally, about the creative process seems to recognize the concept of making to know. It resonates as much with those who consider themselves artists or designers as it does with those who would never identify as professional creatives. It's a concept that can be applied to discovery and learning on many levels; it is relevant to life and spiritual growth and, for some people, to their most personal insights. When I have asked people about it, the typical response has been: "It makes total sense to me, and I'm amazed that I have never defined it that way. My work and my life can be described as a make-to-know process."

I wondered why, if making to know is such a common experience, so few of us identify or name it. To be sure, the trial-and-error nature of creativity finds its way into much of the discourse about how people engage as artists and designers.[6] But no one, to my knowledge, has specifically recognized with precision the relationship of making and knowing, or conducted a deeper study of its implications.[7] Why is this way of thinking largely uncharted? Is there a more dominant counter-narrative that shapes the conversation?

To address these questions, it may be helpful to examine more closely an idea I alluded to earlier: the widespread belief that artists possess some kind of extraordinary vision that comes *before* making. I should say that I use the term "artist" here in a fairly loose sense, embracing various forms of creative expression. Much of this book focuses on the ways in which different people experience the make-to-know concept, and the diversity of their creative practices. But my main purpose is to investigate the traditional narrative that seems to dictate our thinking about creativity.

CREATIVE DISTORTIONS: GENIUS, MADNESS, AND DIVINITY

While the notion of making to know resonated with the people I interviewed, they also readily acknowledged the widespread, seemingly imprinted conviction that artistry is predetermined perception made manifest. I asked them why they thought this idea might have taken root. The responses I received were all over the map.

To some, the explanation was simply that human beings have always been dazzled by great talent. Others talked about economics and the need for gallerists to promote the particular "vision" of an artist in order to sell work. Still others (humorously) suggested that docents and museums draw on the idea of the "inspired" artist as justification for their jobs and institutions, especially when the work itself sometimes seems out of reach or incomprehensible to the average person. And some observed that Western society relies on the myth of great visionaries to validate its cultural heritage. Finally, some speculated on the notion of the artist as healer, prophet, or mystic. Despite these conjectures—and with all appropriate nods to talent—hardly anyone recognized the idea of exceptional vision preceding making as an accurate description of their own creative process.

Accurate or not, this idea of the exalted, visionary artist remains a popular one in Western culture. It is a paradigm, moreover, that for centuries has reflected an entirely male definition of artistry, made by and for men. The history of Western discourse on the creative process is one of clearly defined exceptionalism informed by both race and gender bias. This narrative reinforces an artistic elitism that persists to this day, with consequences for our sense of how artists work.

The historical tropes shaping our sense of creative practice center on three particularly influential ideas of what makes an artist: genius, madness, and divine inspiration. These concepts—sometimes all associated with the same person—have traditionally dominated the discourse on creativity and, I believe, obscured our understanding of make to know.

GENIUS

For much of my early life, I believed that great art was a product of genius. I remember, as a child, hearing apocryphal stories about Beethoven and being dazzled by the idea that he had 'heard' masterpieces in his head. It astonished me to think that someone could be so gifted that, even when he eventually became deaf, he could still hear music internally and bring it forth. What a wonderful tale: the inspired genius created music without the ability to hear. He simply sensed the music, conjured whole masterpieces within himself, and brought them into the world. It was magical and it was beautiful.

Stories about Michelangelo had a similar effect on my understanding of creativity. The master saw the angel in a block of unformed marble— to my young mind, this was a stunning and transformative notion. He saw and then he created. What an extraordinary and formidable skill.

I would venture that many of us have similar early memories of learning about great artistic achievement. The idea of the artist as genius is part of a narrative that reaches a long way back. Historians and scholars have written about the evolution of the concept, notably Darrin McMahon in his book *Divine Fury: A History of Genius*; his analysis elucidates not only the historical preoccupation with the exceptional or prodigious attributes of a select few, but also our ongoing fascination with genius today.

McMahon traces the various definitions of genius that have emerged from its original ancient sense of a "guardian spirit." He discusses the inspired and superhuman figures of the Romantic period. He relates how the idea of the glorified artist finds meaning in relation to the symmetry and order of the neoclassical tradition of the 18th century— a time, McMahon asserts, that brought forth our modern notion of genius "in the bright place of deliverance we call 'the Enlightenment.'"[8] Along the way, he explores meditations of the Christian tradition on the divine-like abilities of geniuses supposedly possessed by the Holy Spirit. Ultimately, McMahon points out an important tension between modern ideas of equality on the one hand and our ongoing preoccupation with genius and extraordinary brilliance on the other. This very tension influences how we think about the creative process and those we believe are capable of engaging in it.

The Harvard professor and Shakespearean scholar Marjorie Garber wrote an article in 2002 entitled "Our Genius Problem." For her, the "problem" is our obsession with genius and our "hope that a genius will come along to save us from our technological, philosophical, spiritual, or aesthetic impasse."[9] Like McMahon, Garber identifies a kind of widespread intoxication with the very concept of genius and a corresponding fixation on the language of superlatives. What McMahon calls "the religion of genius," Garber identifies as an "addiction." In the end, she too offers an important reflection on how that addiction ultimately directs our attention about creativity in problematic ways:

> If we remind ourselves that what is really at stake is creativity and invention; if we can learn to separate the power of ideas from that of personality; then perhaps we will be...less distracted by attempts to lionize the genius as a high-culture hero—as essence rather than force. It's not just another word we need; it's another way of thinking about thinking.[10]

The etymology of the word "genius" is the Latin *genui, genitus*: to bring into being, create, produce. The term also connotes prophetic skill and the male spirit of *gens*, originally meaning "generative power." From

23

the beginning, *genius* is productive, seeding something original; but the origins of that productivity are associated entirely with maleness. In early Roman mythology, *genius* is a personification of male procreative power (specifically of "fathering"), while its counterpart *juno*, associated with marriage and childbirth, links to the female.

In ancient Rome, a *genius* was also a tutelary deity of family and place, a guardian spirit worshiped for generative purposes of all kinds. The term *genius* was often paired with *locus*, or place, to indicate a spirit protective of a given location, a special power associated with a house, district, or even the empire as a whole. The emperor's *genius*, for example, was regarded as the *genius loci* of the Roman Empire.

As McMahon argues, our most recognizable definition of genius today stems from the 18th century and specifically from Immanuel Kant, who explores the relationship of art and genius in *The Critique of Judgment* (1790). As Elizabeth Gilbert neatly pointed out in a 2009 TED talk on creativity, the definition has evolved from a classical notion of "having" genius (as the guardian of place, as external influence, as generative spirit) to our modern idea of "being" a genius (something internal).[11] Kant's work represents a critical turning point in this change.

In the third *Critique*, "Fine Art Is the Art of Genius," Kant asserts that exceptional creative skill is the only satisfactory explanation for the existence of art. His investigation into genius is complex but for our purposes here, it's sufficient to note that Kant's views on genius are inextricably linked with the idea of the exalted artist. In a famous passage of the *Critique*, he writes:

> Genius is the talent (natural endowment) that gives the rule to art. Since talent is an innate productive ability of the artist and as such belongs itself to nature, we could also put it this way: Genius is the innate mental predisposition (*ingenium*) through which nature gives the rule to art.[12]

It is worth taking a moment to wrestle with this short passage because it sums up so much about the genius discourse that persists even today. Kant regards great artists as being naturally endowed with a special prowess that can shape and define creative production. And since, for the philosopher, the individual imagination of the artist is a product of the natural world, genius is the manifestation of a holistic natural system at work. Genius is talent, talent is nature, and nature, *through* talent, "gives the rule to art."

Kant goes on to elaborate that genius lends "soul" or "spirit" to what would otherwise be uninspired work. Genius accesses that which is beyond everyday reason and thought. Genius represents human expression at the highest level; it is nature's magnificent vehicle for expression. For Kant, God was the supreme artist, and God's original act of creativity set in motion the model of our understanding of peak human capacity. Genius is the way toward awe-inspiring creation.

The Romantics picked up on Kant's ideas quite directly. Placing feeling and intuition ahead of reason, focusing on emotion as the source of aesthetic prowess and access to the sublime, they celebrated the individual imagination as something almost heroic. In emphasizing the importance of the personal and the subjective, they relished the expression of human imagination in the context of the natural world. Like Kant, the Romantics concentrated on the concept of *ingenium*, an individual's innate natural qualities. They placed supreme value on creative envisioning; they sought to unify spirit and matter. Emotion, spontaneity, deep expression, the harmony of the mind and the senses—all of these capacities were, in the Romantic mind, venerated as fundamental qualities of the great artist.

By the end of the 18th century and well into the Romantic era, the term "genius" was clearly reserved for the type of human being who possessed godlike abilities, one who possessed an inner daemon or spirit that drove artistic production. This understanding of the godlike artist was strongly associated with notions of preordained vision. Genius distinguished truly original artwork from mere imitation. There was the sublime, and there were inferior human creations. Artistic genius revealed the beauty and mystery of the natural world.

Christine Battersby's book *Gender and Genius: Towards a Feminist Aesthetics* examines the history of genius from a feminist perspective. Battersby seeks to establish a feminist aesthetics that can be applied to the achievements of women artists in the past as well as the present. She points out two gender-related, historically prevalent categories of aesthetics: beauty and sublimity. The former is associated with femininity (and passivity), the latter with masculinity and active genius.[13]

Like Darrin McMahon and Marjorie Garber, Battersby offers a critical analysis of our problematic relationship with genius throughout history and how it has affected the cultural conversation about creativity. The feminist perspective of her work sheds light on a bias of history that excludes women from artistic life. The effects of this bias persist, continuing to limit our understanding of how creativity works and sustaining the notion of the artist as a godlike male figure, making his sublime vision manifest.

The fixation with genius persisted through the 19th century and continues today. Despite—or perhaps because of—the narrowness of the definition, with its principally male and white historical attributes, it seems we cannot rid ourselves of this fascination. There are countless self-help resources on how to become a genius yourself, or shape your child into one. There's an abundance of contemporary films about geniuses: *A Beautiful Mind, Amadeus, Good Will Hunting, The Theory of Everything, The Imitation Game, Hidden Figures, Frida, The Aeronauts.* Sporting heroes like Wayne Gretzky, Michael Jordan, or Lionel Messi are routinely referred to as geniuses. Recent publications on genius include such volumes as Janice Kaplan's *The Genius of Women* (2020) as well as *The Hidden Habits of Genius* by Craig Wright (2020).[14] The prolific critic Harold Bloom wrote a book entitled *Genius* (2002), identifying what he regarded as the hundred greatest minds in history.[15] David Shenk's *The Genius in All of Us* (2010) discusses current discoveries in cognitive science, genetics, and biology suggesting that even if we are not born with genius, we can develop and nurture it under the right circumstances.[16] The MacArthur Foundation's Fellows Program is known for its generous prizes, unofficially dubbed "genius grants," awarded to individuals exhibiting "extraordinary creativity." It's not possible to apply for one of these grants; you have to be nominated. Cofounder John D. MacArthur was direct about his purpose: "Our aim is to support individual genius and to free those people from the bureaucratic pettiness of academe."[17]

We are hooked. As Marjorie Garber makes abundantly clear, we long for genius in our world. We worship it. We want to believe in the exceptional, and in that which transcends routine human capacity. When we see the remarkable, we want to delight in it.

I wonder what we might learn by turning our attention away from the dazzle of genius to a different kind of astonishment about the creative process. Would that pivot open up a new way of looking at human achievement and discovery? I am not denying that there are brilliant individuals among us, nor suggesting that genius is an illusion. I am arguing, however, that the dominant concept of artistic genius can restrict our idea of creativity and, significantly, our sense of what lies behind the production of great work and innovation. Even though the concept of knowing through making might be intuitive, it isn't a prominent part of the creative discourse today. It tends to be eclipsed by popular assumptions about genius, vision, and inspiration—assumptions that have fostered a narrow understanding of the revelatory nature of creative making.

MADNESS

There has never been great talent without
some touch of madness.
—ARISTOTLE, ATTRIBUTED BY SENECA[18]

The narrative of exceptional artistry extends beyond genius. The figure of the artist, at least in the West, has been even more strongly associated with madness, melancholy, and bizarre behavior. The artist's story is one of brooding eccentricity or manic energy that comes with prodigious vision.

This idea of the mad artist goes back at least as far as Plato. His theory of poetical enthusiasm (from the Greek *entheos*, "the god within") is an early depiction of the creative individual as possessed and abnormal. The crazed poet resembled the frenzied participants of Bacchic revels, seemingly in a state of ecstasy (*ex-stasis*, "outside of the self"). For Plato, madness existed independently of the confines of rationality and was therefore distant from fundamental Truth. The illusory—which he defined precisely as that which is not a product of reason alone—was dangerous. In *The Republic*, Plato banished the poets from the just world of the philosopher king.

Alfred North Whitehead famously stated that "philosophy is a series of footnotes to Plato," and perhaps there is a case for extending that description to our ideas about art as well. Have we simply adopted Plato's description of the mad artist, but reversed its negative consequences? I think we have, and this is our defense: far from steering us away from truth and reality, the artist, even if mad, can provide us with deep insights into the world and human existence precisely *because* they are different and strange. Either way, the conversation about madness endures.

There is plenty of further evidence that Westerners have historically been, and continue to be, preoccupied by the idea of the eccentric or mad artist. Countless painters and sculptors have either self-reported on or sparked written accounts about their bizarre and unusual behavior; again, Michelangelo is an example. As Margot and Rudolf Wittkower point out in *Born Under Saturn: The Character and Conduct of Artists:*

> Michelangelo's demonic frenzy of creation...and the total neglect of decorum in his personal appearance and daily life—all this puzzled his contemporaries as much as it did posterity....He has been called avaricious and generous; superhuman and puerile; modest and vain; violent, suspicious, jealous, misanthropic, extravagant, tormented, bizarre, and terrible....[19]

Accounts of the master, self-reported and otherwise (according to the Wittkowers), suggest unquestionably that he was a man tormented by melancholy and isolation. He was brilliant. But he was different, separate, strange.

The artist is mad. The artist suffers. There exists an ancient text spuriously attributed to Aristotle (it was probably one of his students) called *The Problems*, in which the author connects creativity and the arts with a "melancholy temperament." Vincent van Gogh is all the more fascinating to many of us for having cut off his ear. Sylvia Plath captivates us as a brilliant poet who committed suicide by putting her head in a gas oven. Antonin Artaud's suffering and mental anguish became the vital energy behind his work in the theater. Biographies of Ernest Hemingway tell of the deep disquiet that led him to take his own life. Robert Schumann had manic episodes while creating his most brilliant compositions. Debilitating mental illnesses have been attributed to Lord Byron, to Herman Melville, to Virginia Woolf.

The particular relationship of creativity to the contemporary diagnosis of bipolar disorder is an intriguing one that echoes the notion of ecstasy discussed by Plato. In today's language, we talk about a prolific state of manic excitement in which the individual feels a certain level of power and euphoria. How many films of our time explore the relationship between outsized talent and insanity or the unstable personality? Think of the portrayal of John Nash in *A Beautiful Mind* (2001), Ray Charles in *Ray* (2004), Johnny Cash in *Walk the Line* (2005), or David Helfgott in *Shine* (1996). Popular culture displays a persistent interest in the aberrant behavior of artists and people of great creative skill. It is not difficult to understand why we might have accepted the notion that madness is a key characteristic of the artist. But it has skewed our thinking about creativity.

DIVINE INSPIRATION

It seems that poetic inspiration has in it something
too sublime for the common nature of man.
—VICTOR HUGO[20]

Along with talent and genius there sometimes comes a precariously balanced personality, complicated even further by an association with divinity. Not only did the Renaissance idea of the artist have roots in the Platonic notion of the possessed and inspired, but it was informed as well by the notion of *il divino artista*, the divine artist, echoing the fundamental idea of God as artist and architect of the universe. The artist is both divorced from the normal rank and file of humanity, and associated with the divine.

This association goes back to Homer calling on the Muse to sing through the Bard to tell the story of Achilles or Odysseus: "Sing to me of the man, Muse, the man of twists and turns."[21] The Bard channeled the divinity of the Muse. It was magic. It was inspiration. The etymology of the word "inspiration" is "to breathe into," conjuring images of the gods breathing the creative spirit into the storyteller or poet: artists were part of a divinely chosen elite. The idea of the Muse is the most familiar form of divine inspiration and has persisted for thousands of years, giving us the root for the modern word *museum*.

The Muses in Greek mythology were nine sister goddesses of music, poetry, arts, and sciences. They were the source of knowledge itself. There are multiple accounts and descriptions of the Muses as well as debates on their number (some say three, others nine) and their individual names. Later, the term "muse" came to refer to someone or something that inspires a musician, a writer, or an artist. The implication is clear—the knowing is not in the making. It comes instead from outside, perhaps from a divine force communicating through chosen mortals.

The concept of divine inspiration is certainly not specific to Western culture but is familiar in Asian, Native American, and Mayan cultures too. It represents yet another way in which human beings have traditionally associated artistry with special access to something superhuman. Today, even if we no longer literally believe that great creative work has its origins in the divine, some aspects of that idea still persist. We are often tempted to speak of artistic excellence as something mystical or otherworldly, the preserve of only a select few among us. They are special and different, possessed of abilities the rest of us lack. Their creative work is the result of these mysterious gifts rather than a product of making, or of tenacity and grit.

There exists an interesting contemporary twist to the role of the muse in creative life. Instead of summoning the goddess mystically to speak through oneself, one must work hard to prepare for inspiration. As Isabel Allende put it: "Show up, show up, show up, and after a while the muse shows up, too."[22] Or, in the words of Ursula K. Le Guin, "All makers must leave room for the acts of the spirit. But they have to work hard and carefully, and wait patiently, to deserve them."[23] Both of these quotes reflect an interesting turn from ideas of superhuman capacity, born of nature, talent, and supreme ability, toward the notion of hard work itself or readiness to "show up" for the task. With this more contemporary concept we are teetering on the brink of defining the creative process as a presence, a grind, a way to inspiration and discovery that is theoretically open to anyone. The focus shifts from the inspiring deity to the actual process of making great work. Curiously, however, the stronghold of the muse or "the spirit" persists, even for Allende and Le Guin. For all that the notion of discovery through acts of making and creativity might resonate with many of us, we are nonetheless tethered to a notion of the artist as a separate, glorified figure, a celebrated freak.

This idea of the inspired (divinely or otherwise) artist has consequence. It influences how we educate not only professional artists and designers, but our children as well. It shapes our thinking about leadership and our obsession with visionaries. It affects how we regard entrepreneurs, characterizing them as prophetic readers of the future when in fact, most of them—at least, the individuals I have interviewed— identify as grinders and people open to failure, paving a road to discovery.

Building on this long-established association of the artist with divinity, one might even extend the analogy to argue that popular culture holds a "creationist" view of artistic practice. The artist mimics the attributes of a Creator, possessing all knowledge from the start, knowing exactly how each moment in each part of the creation will unfold. We want to deify the creators in our midst, to think of them as having godlike powers to hold vision and to make that vision manifest. We tend to think about the creative process as a creationist might think about the history of the world. Contrast this idea with the Darwinian notion of natural selection, which posits a complex process of evolution in which the strong survive.

The creationist language associated with artistry betrays a largely misguided sensibility. In almost every conversation I have had with artists and designers, the language used about process is not creationist, but much closer to that of natural selection. Most artists and designers don't experience the vision before the making. They speak of "working through," "drawing through," "sketching through," "improvising through," "writing through," "sculpting through" their ideas in the process of developing and making work. Some ideas produced along the way are strong and some are not. The strong, as in natural selection, tend to survive.

A PERSONAL MAKE-TO-KNOW JOURNEY

There is probably no better way for me to convey the essence of make to know than to personalize it: to explain how significant it has been, and continues to be, in my own life. I have already touched on how different aspects of my work reflect this. But a little more of my own story might demonstrate why I am so passionate about the concept of make to know, and why I believe it is so important.

My ideas about unreachable artistic genius made my own creative life as a child challenging to access. How could I ever take myself seriously as an artist, when I knew I had no exceptional abilities? To me, the creative world was a place full of colorful, even notorious characters: people I studied at school or celebrities I observed in popular culture. I remember particularly my experience of music and my clear sense of the unfathomable genius of musicians I enjoyed. I played a little guitar and piano and tried to imitate them. In the end, however, it was, for me, just a hobby, an indulgence. I firmly believed that real creativity was out of reach, reserved for the select few.

And yet, there was one endeavor that had a different effect on me—the theater. I have memories of myself in elementary school loving any and all projects that had to do with performance. They nurtured me. I recall thinking I was particularly good at memorization, but in retrospect I suspect that had more to do with the confidence I was gaining through being on the stage. This excitement carried me through much of high school, but I never thought to pursue it beyond that stage. I didn't have the "genius" for it. I wasn't "creative." I entered college with a firm idea that the humanities, not the arts, would be my focus.

That conviction dissolved when I met a great teacher, Francis Martineau, with whom I studied literature at the University of Toronto. We read the likes of Samuel Beckett, Virginia Woolf, Carson McCullers, Eugene O'Neill, and Bertolt Brecht. I particularly loved reading plays with him. He was clearly a man of the theater as well as a lover of literature, and his passion sparked something in me. At some point I discovered that this teacher was also the head of the drama program at the university. He encouraged me to get involved. I auditioned for one of the plays, and the director cast me.

I enjoyed my involvement in the drama program, but I quickly learned that I wasn't a very good actor. I was too much in my head, critiquing myself at every turn. That's death for a performer. It blocks the full-body participation at the core of acting. I remember Martineau telling me that my acting was "from the neck up," and he was right. But the real problem, in hindsight, was that I couldn't get into a rhythm of make to know in performance. Ironically, my work suffered because I was over-prepared, and in the wrong way. I went into each rehearsal with a "vision" of the character. Every time I deviated from that vision during the course of a rehearsal, I engaged an overactive brain. Neck up, indeed. I was terrible at it.

Fortunately, Martineau also taught a course in directing for the theater, and he had a very specific approach to that course. There was no theoretical preparation. His attitude was simply this: If you want to direct, jump in and direct something. It's the only way to learn it, to know it, and to understand what questions to ask as you go more fully into the art. It was perfect for me and for the way I learn. It was a make-to-know pedagogy.

Working as a director represented the first time in my life that I had truly experienced how it felt to be creative in the deepest way. I arrived at that point of realization, however, via an unexpected route. My first assignment in the class was to direct a short one-act play, and I chose a comedic romp by Anton Chekhov called *The Boor*. I can say with complete honesty that I had no idea what I was doing. I did cast the play, and I scheduled the first rehearsal. I had no clue, however, what I was going to do in that rehearsal. I didn't know how to prepare. I read books. Talked to friends. But it all seemed mysterious to me.

I walked into the space and almost immediately experienced a kind of transformation. I cannot explain it entirely except to say that something of necessity descended upon me when I began that session. We read text out loud. We talked about character. We got up and moved around. We laughed about ideas. We physicalized responses to the play. It was completely natural for me to work in that context and then to stage the play. Actors in space. Batting around ideas. Asking questions. Movement. Sound. Facial expression. By engaging in real activity on a real stage, I knew exactly what I wanted to do. I was *making*, theatrically speaking. I didn't know how to explain any of it at the time. But in certain ways, I look at *The Boor* as a milestone in my creative life.

Something else happened during my work on *The Boor*. I remember struggling with the end of the play; it was awkward, out of rhythm, not right. The harder I tried, the worse it got. But then another surprise. I had a dream (which to this day I remember distinctly) in which Charlie Chaplin appeared to me. I dreamed that the ending of the play needed to take on the quality of a silent movie; I needed to conclude Chekhov's brilliant romp in the spirit of Chaplin, with a live soundtrack (it was a violin in my dream) similar to what one might hear at a screening of a silent film. Everything was there in the dream. This experience might sound like a contradiction of make to know; it might resemble, instead, a "vision" (perhaps mad) that guided the way. But, thanks to the artists and designers I interviewed, I now view the dream very differently.

Creative ideas come to us in odd ways and at unexpected moments, and we need to understand "making" as a multifaceted activity on a broad spectrum. The makers I interviewed quite often talked about discoveries that surfaced at times when they were not focused on the work itself. In fact, the single most frequent statement from all artists and designers with whom I spoke was: "The idea came to me in the shower." Others referenced similar experiences while driving or listening to music—or dreaming. Are these seemingly out-of-context flashes part of make to know? The people I interviewed seem to think they are. They expressed repeatedly that when they are deep in a creative project, something takes over. It feels as if everything they do becomes part of the process, an extended mode of making, even (or perhaps especially) while they sleep. It's really only a matter of circumstance as to how the discovery might arise.

After the Chaplin dream, I cut all lines of *The Boor* in the last several pages of the text, found a violinist, and staged the conclusion—wordless—to music. It worked. And with the addition of the violin, I had a new element; I could explore other ways of using the instrument in other parts of the show. The instrument became a third character. None of those choices emerged out of any "vision"; I discovered them as I made the play.

The experience of directing *The Boor* changed my life, opening up a path to a career in the theater. I can't say it was the first time that I was able to know something from making it, but it was certainly the beginning of any conscious understanding of how that process works in my life. Since then, the same fundamental process has been repeated in many other productions I have directed, and it has manifested in other ways as well. I wrote a book on filmic adaptations of Shakespeare's plays, and much of that creative experience parallels my work as a theater director.[25] At the beginning, I was uncertain about what I wanted to say. What I did have was a rich and driving question I wished to address (and I deliberately use the word "address" rather than "answer"). It was a question that opened the way into the unknown; the actual writing, on the other hand, was what gave me access to my thoughts.

Many of the artists I've interviewed in the last few years talk about a "gateway" into the making process. For me, I had a central question; others call it an urge, an impulse, a generative idea, a notion, a frame, or a riddle. It can even be a brief, in the design world. Through our conversations, I learned how critically important this point of entry is to many artists, and just how fundamentally different it is from a "vision."

With the Shakespeare book, my point of entry was to ask how the films could serve as a critical tool for understanding the plays—in other words, how could the camera take us on a journey through Shakespeare's work that might open insights that reading or seeing a stage production could never reveal? That generative question was important, as was the careful study of the films themselves. But only as I wrote my way through it did my ideas come to me. As with the experience of directing *The Boor*, I had to embark on the journey in order to know anything at all about the thing I was trying to make and who I was in the making of it.

The story of my work in academic settings has some similar elements. I had served on the faculty of the Dramatic Art Department at the University of California, Berkeley, for several years and was up for tenure. In that year of my review, the university hired a well-known theater artist and scholar to lead our department. He came from New York and was scheduled to take over as chair six months after his arrival. What quickly became clear was that this brilliant, somewhat quirky man did not possess the skills that would make him a good leader. He was an interesting colleague but not a competent manager. The dean looked around at the other prospects and decided that I, the newly tenured faculty member of the department, would be appointed chair instead.

As on that first day of rehearsal for *The Boor*, I took on this assignment with deep uncertainty. But again, I went into the breach and experienced a transformation. Once in the role, I learned not only what it might mean to lead this academic department, but also that there existed a fundamental part of me with which that kind of work resonated deeply. I grew to know something of myself, a part of me that came alive in leadership, and this new understanding set yet another path for my career. Through the process of "making leadership," I came to know what I wanted to do, both with the department and with this new aspect of my career.

The same pattern of accident and deep-end learning can be traced in my work in teaching and ultimately as a college president. Each step came as a surprise, with accompanying insecurities and transformation. I entered spaces of unknowing; I responded to necessity; I began to "make" until the process revealed something I could never have otherwise known.

THE SCAFFOLDING OF MAKING

I want to caution against any misunderstanding of this personal journey, or the make-to-know process in general, as being about taking on projects without the necessary background or preparation. Like anyone else, I faced the challenges that came my way with a set of experiences behind me: an education, a developing skill set, particular interests, ethics, beliefs, and priorities. The make-to-know concept has nothing to do with winging it, or making things up as we go along. On the contrary, as I hope will become clear throughout this book, there is a deep relationship between discipline, skill, and focus on the one hand and the kind of discovery that emerges through the creative process on the other. The central point is this: the experience and skill we bring to our projects forms the scaffolding on which we stand as we reach for something in a world that is, at that moment, uncertain. Until we are in the actual process of creating it, we can't fully know what it will be.

My personal history reflects some of the principles and practices that have shaped my life. But it only scratches the surface of this complex and perhaps misunderstood process of making and discovery—of knowing. In conversations about make to know, many people compare it to John Dewey's concept of learning by doing. This is, to a certain extent, an apt association. But Dewey's notion is only a slice of a larger idea I wish to explore, one that I hope will shed light on who we are as a creative species.

Curiously, my experience as president of ArtCenter College of Design over the last decade is the very thing that reignited my sense of make to know and that ultimately compelled me to write this book. The core educational philosophy of this great school can be summed up as "make to know." It teaches through a project-based curriculum and a philosophy of applied learning. Reflection and theory follow the project, and the questions asked are born of making. Indeed, we teach the skill that forms the scaffolding, as well as the courage to reach and explore the unknown. Every day I witness brilliant and astonishingly talented students emerge as artists and designers through this same make-to-know process.

In addition to my own experience of making and knowing, my way into understanding the dimensions and nuances of the concept has come through conversations with writers, artists, and designers. This is not an epistemological study with a philosophical bent; rather, my goal has been to better understand how different creative individuals talk about their common experience of knowing through making. All of my interviewees are professional creatives with established reputations for their original work—influential people who have made an impact on the world. Their insights take us far beyond the obvious and into a fascinating exploration of the creative process itself.

A LOCAL HABITATION AND A NAME

In a well-known speech in the fifth act of Shakespeare's *A Midsummer Night's Dream*, the character Theseus meditates on the strange and, to him, unsettling capacity of the lunatic, lover, and poet to fabricate through imagination what others cannot see. But one can easily extrapolate from Theseus's perspective to see not a madness to dismiss, but a power and strength to celebrate.

> The lunatic, the lover, and the poet
> Are of imagination all compact.
> One sees more devils than vast hell can hold—
> That is the madman. The lover, all as frantic,
> Sees Helen's beauty in a brow of Egypt.
> The poet's eye, in fine frenzy rolling,
> Doth glance from heaven to Earth, from Earth to heaven.
> And as imagination bodies forth
> The forms of things unknown, the poet's pen
> Turns them to shapes and gives to airy nothing
> A local habitation and a name.
>
> (ACT V, SCENE 1, 7–18)

My purpose in this book is to explore what can only be "forms unknown" until "imagination bodies forth" their shape in creative pursuit and gives them "a local habitation and a name." It is, ultimately, a meditation on the human capacity to know through making.

Chapter 2

ENTERING UNCERTAINTY: REVELATIONS OF THE BLANK PAGE

You begin every book as an amateur....Gradually, by writing sentence after sentence, the book, as it were, reveals itself to you... Each and every sentence is a revelation.
—PHILIP ROTH[1]

No poet can know what his poem is going to be like until he has written it.
—W.H. AUDEN[2]

To know what you're going to draw, you have to begin drawing.
—PABLO PICASSO[3]

The literal and figurative blank page. We have all faced it. To some of us, confronting that ocean of possibility can be terrifying, filling us with doubt and anxiety. How will I conjure the first words of this novel? How will I break through? This vast, empty canvas—where do I start? How do I find the first notes for this song, its rhythmic structure? My client gave me a brief—how do I even begin to find the innovative solution they need?

Perhaps I should clean out those drawers in my desk first. I haven't called my mother in a few days. You know, I'm actually pretty hungry.

The first fundamental principle of make to know is this: We begin our creative journeys by entering uncertainty, a space brimming at once with opportunity and intimidating emptiness. That fabled blank page can be a painful, even paralyzing, prospect—but according to the artists and designers I've interviewed for this book, entering uncertainty, despite the apprehension it may cause, can also be empowering and ultimately revelatory. How, then, do we engage with that uncertainty? Where do we find the courage to enter the unknown, and how do we do it? What does that space feel like? What happens once we're inside it?

While conducting the interviews, I noticed that writers—of all stripes—are particularly skilled at addressing these questions, and in this chapter I focus much of my attention on their reflections. To deepen the conversation, however, I also weave in the work of practitioners in the fields of installation art, film, and screenwriting, and explore through that work several important nuances of what it means to enter uncertainty.

Writers quite literally know what the blank page experience is all about. In fact, they are often surprisingly accepting of the idea that they will feel lost for a while at the beginning of a project. There are countless analogies about writing, but the following description, conveyed to me by novelist and poet Dennis Phillips, is fairly typical: "When you begin it's like you're in the middle of the ocean on a raft and you don't have a compass, so you may as well just begin to paddle one way and not the other—because you just don't know where you are or where you are going."

In a 2017 interview, novelist Nicole Krauss reflected on her writing process and spoke about "the power of entering a space of the unknown." She actually described the experience as "calming," from which I gathered a sense of focus and readiness to embark on a journey to find, as she put it, "coherence on the other side."[4] What Krauss finds calming, other writers experience as uneasiness. Either way, they all convey a central recognition and acceptance of entering the unknown and setting out on a journey of possibility.

Relevant here is the concept of "negative capability," coined by the Romantic poet John Keats in a letter written in 1817 to his brother about William Shakespeare. The idea has interesting parallels with the way many writers talk today about entering into the creative space of the unknown. Keats wanted to celebrate the artist or poet as one "capable of being in uncertainties, mysteries, doubts, without any irritable reaching after fact and reason."[5] He deeply admired the capacity of the artist to create a thing of beauty that suspends resolution and accommodates ambiguity.

The idea of negative capability has found its way over time into the discourse surrounding art and poetry, and even into the social sciences.[6] Baudelaire described negative capability as "an ego a-thirst for the non-ego."[7] John Dewey cited the idea as having influenced his writings on philosophical pragmatism; he saw Keats's concept as a "psychology of productive thought."[8] In the same spirit, the 20th-century British psychoanalyst Wilfred Bion saw the richness of Keats's concept as pertinent to possibilities of breakthrough and transformation in psychotherapy. He stressed the importance of the patient entering a state of the unrecognized and un-navigated—"without memory or desire."[9] Similarly, Zen Buddhist philosophy speaks of the concept of *Satori*, variously translated from the Japanese as awakening, comprehension, understanding, or sudden insight. Interestingly, finding that moment can only happen when it is preceded by doubt and uncertainty: "The antecedent stages to *Satori*: quest, search, ripening and explosion. The 'quest' stage is accompanied by a strong feeling of uneasiness, resembling the capacity to practice negative capability while the mind is in a state of 'uncertainties, mysteries and doubts.'"[10] In all these examples, the common denominator is the experience of discovery that comes from yielding to the unknown. In a space not readily defined, possibility begins.

Negative capability (and entering uncertainty) is not about passive resignation, ignorance, or insecurity. It is, importantly, an active pursuit. It brings to mind what philosopher Donald Schön has memorably called "an epistemology of practice implicit in the artistic, intuitive processes which some practitioners...bring to situations of uncertainty..."[11] Many of the individuals I interviewed mentioned the creative potential inherent in being unsure. Some insisted that they needed it. But all emphasized feeling energized by the process of finding the way.

POINTS OF ENTRY

Your triggering subjects are those that ignite your need for words....Your words used your way will generate your meanings....Your way of writing locates, even creates, your inner life.
—RICHARD HUGO[12]

How does the writer begin? To borrow Richard Hugo's term, what are the "triggering subjects," the points of entry? I put this question to a number of different writers. It's one thing to enter a space of uncertainty, but what sets the process in motion? Is it a big bang? A small inkling? The descriptions vary. A central life question will trigger some writers; a routine, banal idea will activate others. Entry points might come from a random observation, an isolated experience, an emotional stirring, a joke, a word, an idea for a narrative voice, a rhythmic urge, or simply "showing up."

Novelist Aimee Bender tells me that her point of entry is actually physical, not intellectual or emotional. "I write every day. I have a very firm structure; I simply commit to an hour and a half of sitting there. The joke—but it was true for me—is that the first time I tied my leg to the chair." The description of her process echoes the amusing and perhaps apocryphal stories about Victor Hugo locking himself in his study and writing naked. He would, apparently, give his clothes to his servants with strict orders not to give them back until he completed a substantial amount of writing.

Bender is more balanced in her practice: she simply holds the scheduled ninety minutes as sacred, writing or not. She needs to be physically present; for her, entry into the creative act is carving out time. "And I write down when an hour and a half will be up. And then that will be that. Later I read the essay on boredom by [psychoanalyst] Adam Phillips. He talks about cultivating boredom as a creative space. My writing really changed. I was restless. I was restless and bored but had this rule; the writing got much looser and stranger, and I got a lot of work done. And that has held me through all the books I've written."

The furniture designer and educator Rosanne Somerson echoes Bender's thoughts about boredom as an entry into creative space. She relays to me an exercise she has often conducted with her students to encourage new levels of discovery. She requires them simply to sit and sketch for an hour and forbids them to leave their chairs or to take any break whatsoever. Her interest is in what might emerge when the individual endures restlessness and even anxiety. She recognizes discomfort itself as a fertile context for ideas: "Our body is very adept at knowing how to prevent us from going into places that are not comfortable, so finding a way to get into that place when you are utterly bored is sometimes the most beautiful way to instigate a new kind of thought process, one that takes you into a whole new realm." Somerson is teaching a discipline of making, and she is broadening its definition to include showing up in a moment of uneasiness. It's another point of entry. The maker, like someone practicing mindful meditation, enters a space of uncertainty by setting up the opportunity to observe, without judgment, what might come through being present in the moment, even amidst (or because of) feelings of discomfort and restlessness.

In her TED talk on creativity, novelist Amy Tan asserts that she enters a world of uncertainty from a place of moral ambiguity which is, for her, a source of some of her deepest questions. She specifies that engaging a central question is her point of access. "I get these hints, these clues....and what I need, in effect, is a focus. And when I have the question, it is a focus. And all these things that seem to be flotsam and jetsam in life actually go through that question, and what happens is those particular things become relevant."[13]

Poet and novelist Joseph Di Prisco speaks of entering with a simple notion or imprecise idea and then, through the act of writing itself, discovering a narrative voice that guides him, a voice that he conjures *through* the writing: "There is a way, when you are writing, that you find your narrator's story and his or her voice is taking you down a path. And you have to follow that. You have to listen to that voice. All the clues are there."

The story of how Tom Stern developed his novel *My Vanishing Twin* offers insight into his encounter with the unknown and his entry point into this mysterious place of creative discovery.[14] "I simply began to write about a character," Stern tells me. "I'm always observing people, reading people, thinking about people, and trying to understand. I spend a lot of time trying to think about the difference between myself and some other person and how we wind up in the places we do." When he does begin the writing, no matter what observation triggered his search, he very deliberately tries to eradicate any preconceived expectations of where he might be heading. For him, expecting to manifest a certain idea (or even reach a certain goal) eclipses the make to know of writing. If he comes to the creative process with expectations, there is a danger that he will work toward fulfilling those expectations instead of remaining open to what the writing might reveal.

Amy Tan crystallizes this very point compellingly with what she calls "the terrible and dreaded observer effect." "You're looking for something," she warns, "and you know...you're looking at it in a different way, and you're trying to really look for the 'about-ness'.... And if you try too hard, then you will only write 'the about.' You won't discover anything." Tan characterizes the creative process not as a search for something preconceived, but as a discipline that creates the conditions for invention.

With *My Vanishing Twin*, Stern simply started writing about his protagonist. He wrote to get to know his character, to understand his behavior—all through the process, as he put it, of "moving words around," writing through it. In this particular instance, he discovered a character who was struggling with his own stasis, someone who had compromised just about everything in his life.

"Can you tell me why that figure was of interest?" I ask.

"I can't. I don't know why that was a compelling kind of character beat or note for me; it just was." He wrote pages and pages about this figure. And then, at a certain point, he began to think about what it would take to shock the character into some sort of new or different action in his life. That question of shock and transformation hovered for Stern but, eventually, he needed to leave the pages of writing and clear his mind. He needed to do something else.

"What happened when you left it, when you took that break?"

"That's when the central image came. I was sitting on my bed; my wife was asleep next to me. Just sitting there before I went to sleep, there came the image of this man who is pregnant with—a *man* who is *pregnant*! And simultaneously another image came to mind of this malformed, misshapen little person. And I remember initially thinking about the relationship between these two images—the pregnant man and the misshapen figure. And then out of nowhere the answer came that they were brothers. And I realized that I was looking at a story about a guy who was pregnant with his own twin brother. I was incredulous, saying that to myself. But I also remember another internal voice—'yeah, that's right, and now the job is to figure out what the hell it's about.'"

There is much to uncover about the process Stern describes. Quite obviously, he is wholly in that place of uncertainty when he begins. With an entry point triggered by an observation in the world, a question about a character, he finds himself on that metaphorical raft in the middle of the ocean. He begins to paddle in a direction, moving through the vast unknown to the known (or, perhaps more accurately, to a place of knowing more). His practice brings him to a pivotal point of insight not, in this instance, at a moment *in the midst* of writing but at a moment when he is doing something else—sitting on his bed, opening up a space for an idea to surface. There is creative power in a pause.

Repeatedly, the people I interview describe what amounts to a continuum of making that extends beyond the specific act itself, encompassing times when they are not (seemingly) directly occupied with the work. It is as if artists engaging in a project enter an expanded state of possibility. Insight emerges, sometimes, through the direct act of doing; other times it comes in retreat. Making, it turns out, is part of a spectrum of engagement. Discovery is not fundamentally something we can control; we can only construct the circumstances for its realization.

Both Stern and Bender insist on everyday practice as an essential part of the make-to-know experience. Stern tells of a pivotal moment in his career when he was studying under the great writer and teacher Elie Weisel. In a one-on-one conference, Weisel said to him quite directly: "I'll give you one piece of advice. If you call yourself a writer and if you take yourself seriously, you will sit down every single day and you will make the time to write. And it doesn't matter if it's for twenty minutes and complete garbage or if it's for four hours of divine inspiration—you'll just write it down."

"That was twenty years ago," he tells me. "I've written every single day of my life since then."

The practice of writing in regular rhythm is itself a way into this world of the unknown. It is a kind of preparation. Some writers talk about writing as exercising a muscle. The analogy is apt. Writers get in shape with writing like athletes get in shape with their bodies. What is painful and inflexible at the beginning eventually becomes stronger, supple, even graceful. The discipline of writing every day is the training for all that may come. The practice is the preparation and is essential if a writer is to thrive in a place of uncertainty, a place of creative discovery.

Chris Kraus tells a thought-provoking story about how her epistolary novel *I Love Dick* came into being. The entry point into the world of the unknown was, for Kraus, a question about what she considered a failed career as an independent experimental filmmaker. When she completed her final film, *Gravity and Grace*, a project that she worked on for two and a half years and that required personal financial investment, she eventually had to face the sad reality that very few people would ever see it. Ultimately, it languished.

"It was the last film I made. After that, I swore that I would never make another film until I discovered why my work had not been successful. And so exploring that question became the work of *I Love Dick*. In my mind, anyway, I wanted to use myself as a case study to discover why my films had been failures."

What Tom Stern explores through the "triggering subject" of character, Kraus examines by way of her own experience. *I Love Dick* takes the form of love letters to another person. The characters are Chris and Sylvere (her then husband and longtime collaborator). Chris and Sylvere work together on love letters to a third party, Dick, who is Dean of Critical Studies at the California Institute of the Arts. Dick never replies to the letters, nor does he rebuff them. The letters just go out. "Writing on the silence," in Kraus's exquisite phrase—a variation on the theme of writing in uncertainty. Dick becomes a blank screen onto which Kraus can project everything, the *tabula rasa* of the imagined listener.

I prod her to go further. "Say more about how that fantasy listener functioned for you."

"It gave me a recipient, someone that I was talking to. In writing programs, they talk about finding your voice. I think what they're really saying is find your audience." By writing letters to Dick, she set up a structure that allowed her to talk to an external figure born of her own internal world, one that for her held certain cultural norms and limitations. In addition, she deliberately used that structure to create a self-reflexive dynamic. "I was determined to become an art historian of my own work. I wanted to take the terrible feelings of shame, failure, and humiliation out of myself and externalize them and look at them in relation to the culture."

"Did you intend *I Love Dick* to be a novel at all? Or was it just personal inquiry?"

"I really thought I was just writing letters to this person, that it was kind of an art project," she tells me.

Writing those letters became a discovery for Kraus that took place on at least two levels. The first was the encounter with herself: wrestling with deep questions of her artistic past as she wrote repeatedly and incessantly to this "perfect listener." But on another level, writing the letters led to the discovery of something larger that eventually took the form of a novel. "I didn't know it was a book until 1997," she says. By that time, she had been writing the letters for a few years. "I went out to the desert with years' worth of folders and copies of the letters. I rented a cabin and played with those letters, edited them a bit, shortened them. I began to shape them into the form of a book. The letters are what made it possible for me to start writing a book that became *I Love Dick*."

Courtney Martin, a blogger and author of several books, talks to me about her creative engagement with generative questions that confront her in everyday life, questions that serve as her points of entry. Like Chris Kraus, Martin speaks of how she navigates the personally unresolved and uncertain *through* her writing. She cites her weekly blog for the website *On Being* as an example of her process: in writing it, she often drives a variety of immediate and pressing issues to a fresh point of consideration. "It is about how I'm living my life. I'm looking for patterns. I'm looking for questions. I'm looking sometimes for just a moment that's interesting."

Martin is a journalist by training, and it is noteworthy to consider how she enters the unknown. She reflects that the journalistic process is typically one of investigation and reporting in the third person. Her inquiries, however, while born of cultural or political questions, are characteristically also deeply subjective. "A traditional journalist," she tells me, "would research something, write about it, but never use the first person. Never use the 'I'."

This combined perspective in her work—the journalist and the personal chronicler—intrigues me. Martin is able to connect in a most unusual way big-picture issues with her own vulnerability, her life questions, her uncertainty. In the end, the conditions she creates for discovery in uncertainty, for working out her own thinking, for finding a way of knowing her point of view through the making/writing of it, is a product of both finely honed research and her own personal courage. Writing makes possible knowing something of the self. In the words of Martin's friend and mentor, the venerable author and teacher Parker Palmer: "Writing is an unfolding of what's going on inside of me as I talk to myself on a pad of paper or a computer, a version of talk therapy that requires neither an appointment nor a fee."[15] Richard Hugo, cited above, extends the point even further: "Your way of writing locates, even creates, your inner life."

In our conversation, Martin focuses on a project she is working on to elucidate her point further. As a mother of young children, she is wrestling with the educational options available to her family, wrestling with issues of class, access, and race in the world of public schools of Northern California. How do even the most liberal and open-minded white middle-class families make choices when it comes to the education of their children? "I'm working on a series right now about public education as an example of how white parents have been the obstacle to integration in many ways in public school systems." The question she raises is certainly pertinent to this moment in our culture, part of a larger societal challenge. Simultaneously, however, she is personally right in the middle of it all, struggling openly with us, with her own situation, with a pressing choice that she herself needs to make regarding her children. The combination is powerful and gives evidence of how Martin engages her creative process not just to know the product of the writing, but how she wants to live as well.

During a conversation about his poetry, Joseph Di Prisco offers a particularly unusual reflection about entering uncertainty.

"How would you describe your entry point into the uncertainty of a poem you set out to write?" I ask him.

"It's a rhythm," he responds. "It's a sound. It's music. Like I feel something and it needs to attach to words."

I love this response, which is unlike anything I have previously heard about entry points. "Can you expand on that?" I ask. "Can you describe the experience in more detail?"

"I have an unsettled feeling. I feel off. I can only discharge that feeling by writing a poem."

It is compelling to speak to a writer sparked by "rhythm" and "uneasiness," one who doesn't have a vision of the poem before he writes it but is compelled by urges, even yearnings. He stresses to me as well that, with his poems, he doesn't "have a case to make."

"I'm not telling the reader what I am thinking about. I want to make the sound beautiful or appropriate to the music/rhythm, appropriate to what I'm writing...I'm not trying to replicate anything. I'm trying to create something."

The distinction illustrates compellingly how make to know shifts our sense of the creative process. It is not so much the replication of an already known notion or vision, but an unfolding of an idea in the making itself.

BUILDING WORLDS AND COSMOLOGIES: A WRITER'S UNCERTAINTY PRINCIPLE

*The important thing is that what we have...is an
aesthetic of making rather than one of expression.*
—GABRIEL JOSIPOVICI[16]

The value of nothing: out of nothing comes something.
—AMY TAN[17]

Having found an entry into this world of uncertainty, what then? What does the writer build within that space that moves the project forward? Amy Tan addresses this question by offering the idea of constructing a cosmology: "I have to develop the cosmology of my own universe as the creator of that universe." It is an environment for making, a framework, however mysterious, that allows the process to unfold.

Tan uses quantum mechanics to elaborate on her metaphor, "which I really don't understand," she confesses, "but I'm still going to use it." It is richly stimulating to think of the cosmology of creativity as energy and dark matter, string theory, particles, and a cosmological constant. It suggests as well parallels with Heisenberg's uncertainty principle, or the extrapolated reality that even the artist cannot know fully the exact position and momentum of the particles of the world they create. Tan needs to surrender to the cosmology of the created universe, even as she makes it. "You don't know what is operating," she explains, "but something is operating there." You can approach knowing only by engaging in it. Tan's exploration of her creative process centers on grappling with that enigmatic operation, playing with ambiguity, probing the mysteries—all through her "focus," or that central question she finds as her point of entry.

That focus, for the novelist, is the filter through which certain very specific issues become relevant. And with that emerging relevance her ideas have a chance to cohere and expand, and the writer suddenly recognizes persistent patterns: "It seems like it is happening all the time." And the making yields amazement: "You think there's a sort of coincidence going on, serendipity, in which you're getting all this help from the universe."

I spoke earlier of a continuum of making, in which creative engagement extends beyond the specific act of writing itself—sitting on a bed
or stepping away. The pause. Chance and coincidence are examples
Tan uses to illustrate that experience. The cosmology of her universe
contains much that would otherwise seem random but, in a larger
spectrum of making, appears purposeful.

"There are also things, quite uncanny, which bring me information
that will help me in the writing of the book...I was once writing a story
that included some kind of detail, period of history, a certain location.
And I needed to find something historically that would match that. And
I took down this book, and I—first page that I flipped it to was exactly
the setting, and the time period, and the kind of character I needed..."

Tan enters a cosmology that is filled with opportunity; it carries
with it the potential of chance, accident, the unpredictable. The creative process is undeniably, for many artists, that central experience of
invention born of the seemingly random. "What are the things that you
get from the universe that you can't really explain?" Tan wonders. "I
have so many instances like this, when I'm writing a story, and I cannot
explain it. Is it because I had the filter that I have such a strong coincidence in writing about these things? Or is it a kind of serendipity that
we cannot explain, like the cosmological constant?"

What Amy Tan helps us understand is the beauty of yielding to the
laws of a cosmology that arises through making itself. In that world,
discoveries happen and mysteries unfold; the writer learns and accesses
a different part of herself, unknown beliefs, ideas unimaginable before
entering. "After being there for a while, and seeing the amazing things
that happen," Tan explains, "you begin to wonder whose beliefs are those
that are in operation in the world, determining how things happen. So
I remained with them, and the more I wrote that story, the more I got
into those beliefs, and I think that's important for me—to take on the
beliefs, because that is where the story is real, and that is where I'm
going to find the answers to how I feel about certain questions that I
have in life."

Tom Stern echoes Tan's point: "Only by going through the various
steps and stages will I ever be able to get to a point where it dawns on

me that this point connects to that point, and I begin to see the shape of things. I have often found myself surprised that I didn't see those connections beforehand—why the hell didn't I see that? For me, there is no other way than through it to make those connections. I don't even know what the action is other than to sit down and move the words around and to work through it."

The very act of finding one's bearings as a writer, or exploring within the laws of a particular cosmology, can often unleash a sense of excitement and prolific creative output. Discovering the way through the unknown is invigorating. Dennis Phillips conveys to me that the very act of writing, of achieving a sense of direction (even momentarily) in an uncertain world, can open the floodgates. He fixes on that exciting moment: "Ah, I know where I am." And it feels like an epiphany, and then suddenly "the words are just pouring out in a way that feels like it's coming from without rather than from within. It's a wonderful feeling. It's an amazing feeling."

The experience Phillips articulates is not uncommon; many writers use similar language that suggests a feeling of something coming from outside the self, something the artist channels. Indeed, many describe what sounds like an out-of-body experience. This may be one reason why so many theories of creativity incorporate notions of divine inspiration. Other writers, however, explain that even though one might feel as if the force is outside of oneself, the act of writing actually taps into "another consciousness—but of the self," as Di Prisco puts it.

Similarly, the psychologist Adam Phillips talks about the act of writing as revealing *surprises* about the self, aspects of our unconscious that remain hidden until the making occurs. Aimee Bender adds a compelling insight: "If you are not surprised or you are not discovering, the reader will probably find the work to be flat or predictable." She cites the novels of Haruki Murakami to illustrate her point. "I can feel in his books a kind of intuitive movement. I can just feel it. And I think that's why I love them so much. And if in another book I find building blocks in place, even expertly moved, like Philip Roth, I can appreciate it and I can value it, but it doesn't go deep. It is a more distant appreciation, but it's not like it's rearranging my interior."

In her metaphor of a multifaceted and complex cosmology, Amy Tan offers an ingenious description of what might develop in the creative realm of uncertainty. Hers is a universe that yields both structure and surprise, the intended and the random, chance and order. It is a context that allows the writer to find both story and self (in a way comparable to Courtney Martin), an architecture of the imagination that reveals artistic form and personal depth. What is most significant about the metaphor in understanding make to know is how her cosmology emerges in the writing itself; it is something the writer experiences simultaneously as product and process. It's not unlike improvisation, where a thing made and a thing discovered are one (an issue I'll return to later). The cosmology in the making becomes the "cosmic theater" within which the narrative unfolds.[18] The writer enters uncertainty but, having entered, finds an expanding universe of gravitational pull, dark matter, and exquisite light—all yielding the opportunity for deep creative invention.

STRUCTURED SPONTANEITY

Exploring the work of installation/film artist Diana Thater deepens our understanding of the maker's relationship to uncertainty, and her projects are particularly interesting to contemplate in comparison to the practice of writers. Thater draws an important distinction between her work in installation and her work in film, two elements that she often blends in the same piece. During our discussion, she offers an intriguing reflection on how uncertainty plays a different role in each part of her work: "I can't blueprint an installation (I have to be in the space even to imagine what it is I'm going to do with it), but I often have to blueprint a film shoot."

Why the disparity? Why does one aspect of Thater's work call on a process distinct from the other? Part of the answer is simply that different disciplines will naturally have different requirements for making in the unknown. A novelist might enter a world of uncertainty with the vaguest of guidelines and the widest possible framework, building structure along the way, in that cosmology of discovery Amy Tan discusses. A filmmaker, however, for practical reasons, may need to develop structure at an earlier stage. Does the making/knowing relationship change as a result? How does entering uncertainty function differently in the film shoot and the installation work?

Before we address these questions, it's important to remember that limitation and structure, in most disciplines, are usually just issues of timing, of the phases of a project that eventually impose increased restriction. The artists and designers with whom I speak are clear on this point: what might begin in the open seas of creation eventually finds its way into the narrows of production. Opening night arrives; the gallery must display the painting; the press sets the layout and text of the book; the designer delivers the product; the architect's design must be ready for construction.

Let us look closely at one of Thater's projects, *As Radical as Reality*: an installation piece centered on filming the world's last male northern white rhino, named Sudan (see page 61). In March 2016, Thater went to Kenya to film her subject. "There are three rhinos left," she tells me in our conversation in October 2017, "two female, one male. And when Sudan dies, the species will be considered extinct because there's no more possibility for reproduction." Sadly, in March 2018, Sudan did die at age forty-five, with all consequences of a lost species; but not before Thater had documented this most beautiful and impressive creature.

When shooting, especially for a project like *As Radical as Reality* with its several challenges and complications, Thater needed a plan, and for the most part she had to stick to that plan. Just as in filmmaking generally, with the business realities of studios, the hiring of technicians, camera people, and an entire cast, there are clear restrictions of process. Time is money. The whole enterprise would be unaffordable (if not impractical) without a great deal of preparation and anticipation of what is to come. How, then, do these constraints affect make to know and the power of spontaneous discovery?

"When I start to make something," Thater tells me, "I have a concept or an image." That concept or image is her entry point into uncertainty, and her early stages of work evolve through a series of playful studio activities that shape her thinking, deepen her idea, and prepare her for a key moment of execution. She generates questions, reads, studies images, imagines possibilities, plays—and uses her studio space to explore and invent. She then formulates a plan necessary for film production.

Specifically, with the project about Sudan, she wrestled with the concept of bringing dignity to the fading moment of a species and grieving its impending loss. As she went through her studio process, she came to know what she wanted. "I decided to film the sun setting over him," she recalls. "The sun setting on a species. That's it. And I wanted Sudan to be this iconic figure. So I decided to shoot him completely in profile."

But even with such a powerful guiding image, what happened when she was actually on location? Were there changes? Did she improvise in the moment? And if so, were those changes minor or substantial? Did she have an opportunity, once there, to recognize something otherwise impossible to know beforehand? The answer, with the Sudan project, is that changes happened in small but significant ways as Thater adapted to such unpredictable factors as the landscape, the light, the relationship of the setting sun to the position of the rhino, and what the animal was doing at a given moment. "During the shoot, I needed to make a decision about moving a camera or creating a different camera angle or shooting distance." One interesting decision on location included the addition of a shot at sunrise to explore a different nuance of light, of perspective and quality of image. "I did end up filming the rhino at both sunrise and sunset, to see what each looked like." That gave her footage that was both product and discovery of the moment.

As Thater and I explore some of her other projects, she tells me about film shoots that were much more spontaneous than *As Radical as Reality* and that uncovered additional nuanced elements of make to know in her work. For her video installation *Chernobyl* (2012), for instance, she went to the location in advance to walk the space. "I went on a go-see," she says. "I spent a full day in Chernobyl and then came back to design the project." In another example, *A Runaway World*, Thater filmed a herd of elephants in Kenya's Chyulu Hills. "I did that shoot of wild free elephants in March 2017. I was tracking them with conservationists and rangers—finding elephants and filming them. In that case, I did not plan what I was going to shoot at all, because I had no idea what I was going to get. I knew what I wanted, but I didn't know what I was going to get."

"Tell me what it means when you say you knew what you wanted,"
I ask.

"There's always the perfect shot. I imagine it. Can I get the perfect shot?"

"Do you see that perfect shot in your mind's eye?"

"Yes, I do. I see it. When I went to Chernobyl, I was filming a herd of
wild horses that were living in this poison environment. And the shot
that I wanted was of one of these wild horses or a herd of wild horses
in the streets of the abandoned city. Who knew if I was going to get this
shot? I arrived, and there were the horses, right there on the street." She
needed to respond to what chance presented. "They were on the street,
and I shot it with the only camera I had in my hand at that moment,
which was a tiny little Leica."

Thater's story is, to me, compelling not so much as an illustration of predetermined vision made manifest, but in what it uncovers
about readiness in the making itself. Her recounting of this moment in
Chernobyl is most powerful in revealing how detailed planning, perhaps
paradoxically, is essential to leveraging the beauty of the fortuitous.
Preparation, discipline, experience: all, as countless musicians teach
us, are necessary elements of great improvisation.

As noted previously, experience, skill, education, and values all form
a kind of scaffolding that supports the artist as they enter uncertainty.
To the elements of that scaffolding, Thater adds the groundwork specific
to a specific project. In both her Chernobyl and Sudan pieces (to varying degrees), what she saw in her mind's eye—that vision—ultimately
became, in the course of making, really a structure for active response
in the moment; a framework that made capturing the spontaneous
possible. As such, another nuance of making (and hence another way of
knowing) surfaces, in the form of preparation to answer and respond to
uncertainty and the *un*planned—making as readiness. As Louis Pasteur
famously put it, "chance favors the prepared mind."

I explore the making/readiness relationship further with Thater
by returning to the story of the elephants in Kenya. "Was creating *A
Runaway World* a similar product of structured spontaneity, of building a kind of readiness? What prepared you to be responsive to the
improvisational nature of dealing with the elephants?"

"All of my experience. Everything I know. All of my experience working with wild animals. And I got the shot, the shot that I imagined." But again, the success of the work came from the preparation, this time with the collaborators she enlisted, and from the willingness to wait for the perfect moment to arrive. "I was shooting with these conservationists, and they knew this swimming pool, which was at the Big Life headquarters where the bull elephants (I was only filming bulls) come in and drink out of the swimming pool. I told the conservationists what I wanted. They recommended that I set up every night, set up in a hide, which is a barrier, so you conceal yourself while filming. And I filmed from hides every night. And I even filmed just sitting on the edge of the swimming pool with the elephants right there. Eventually, I got the shot."

Installation view of Diana Thater's *A Runaway World*
at The Mistake Room, Los Angeles, 2017.

Rebeca Méndez, *CircumSolar, Migration 1*. Installation at 2013
Glow arts event in Santa Monica, California. The work is a
single-channel, 30-minute video projection onto a 25-foot
diameter screen, raised above the sand on a circular truss.

This moment in Thater's story echoes an insight shared with me by
artist Rebeca Méndez. Méndez sees waiting itself as a deeply creative
act. "It's about quieting everything. 'Not knowing' also means that you
cannot always be on the move or in a hurry." She offers an example from
her piece *CircumSolar, Migration 1*, a video project that follows a tiny
four-ounce bird, the Arctic Tern. This bird has the longest migration
of all beings on Earth, flying from the Arctic to the Antarctic and back
again each year. "I am in the Arctic and a lot of waiting happens. It's
part of being in nature. Waiting." She sees the waiting as another way
to come to knowing, to arrive at a point where "you feel nature, with
every part of you, all your senses open, to see things anew." The waiting

58

is also a creative space of solitude. "It's a loneliness that allows me to see the world differently. The waiting is a way of being able to be not only with nature, but with myself, which is the hardest thing. *Being* has been so confused with *doing* something. When I find myself waiting in this very quiet being, what I'm looking for is a dissolution of my sense of self, the sense of my identity, the sense of my boundaries. So, I end up 'becoming with,' right? Becoming with a landscape, becoming with the wind, becoming with the birds, becoming that which I study. So, waiting, waiting, being there, I dissolve."

"Waiting is not, then, something passive," I say.

"Exactly! I'm actively waiting. And it's an action of not knowing and is incredibly scary. And I'm vulnerable in it." Waiting, deceptively and perhaps paradoxically, can be an act of entering uncertainty.

Following her story about waiting for the right shot of the elephants, Thater describes a nuance of this waiting that occurs during a shoot, opening a way to yet further discovery. She compares her work film-ing wild animals to that of "the novelist who experiences characters asserting what they want to say." She talks about structuring a space for the animals ("her characters") to assert themselves, and about how she, in turn, deliberately prepares to listen to them. When she returns to the studio to study the results of a shoot, that same spirit of listen-ing continues as she opens herself to what might surface in the next phase of making. "I look back at the work and I say, okay, what did I do? I take my time, and I always find something revelatory in that process of taking it in." Those revelations then become the basis for her next stage of work, the installation.

A more recognizable process of make to know surfaces in Thater's work during the installation phase. It is in this stage of the process that she uses SketchUp, a 3D modeling program for a range of draw-ing applications (architectural, interior design, landscape architecture, film and video game design). Using this software is a first step toward making the presentation. SketchUp gives her the opportunity to test possibilities, making to know in a digital world. "I start with hand draw-ings and then go to SketchUp to begin mock-ups. I also mock up in big empty spaces. Or I will go to a specific space where the show will take place, if I can, and I will play with the piece in that space. But typically, the work almost always comes out the way I designed it in SketchUp. I love three-dimensional modeling because I come from an architecture background. Working in space and with space comes naturally to me. In that phase of the work, the piece is always changing. Maybe I'll do this. Let me try that. Let me do this. And only through that making process do I find what I want—'ah, now it looks right.'"

When Thater came back from filming Sudan, for example, she went through her process and ultimately designed the installation to show the filmed images on two screens that intersected and projected different perspectives on the rhino, "one from either side of him as the sun was setting." She did this because she "wanted to complicate the profile of the rhino." The more she "made" the design of the installation, the more she knew what that complication entailed. "I wanted to have a subjectivity that greets the viewer's subjectivity on equal ground. So what was important, in the end, was that the rhino be big enough and that his eyes were on the eye level of the viewer. But it was important that the viewer feel smaller. The subjectivity of the rhino is a complex thing. I wanted to find that in choreographing the installation. The work, to me, is like dance in space." The intersecting screens were her solution.

But when she finally tested those intersecting screens, the idea wasn't working for her. And so she engaged in making again. She manipulated things, moved them around, worked with different images, changed the relationships among parts of the whole. At one point in that exploratory process, she decided to flip one of the images on the split screen. "I made it appear backward. It worked. Once one of the images was backward, it worked. I just knew it." She made it. And she knew it.

After Thater understood what it was she wanted to do, colleagues came to see it, and they in turn offered her a language to describe what she had made. She knew it worked, but it was her colleagues who defined it. "'You folded the space' they told me. And they were right, because you see the rhino from both sides simultaneously, and it inverts. 'You managed to fold space in the simplest possible way, just by making these crisscrossed screens.' They were completely right!'"

Diana Thater, *As Radical as Reality*, 2017. Two custom screens,
two video projectors, two media players. Installation view at
The Mistake Room, Los Angeles.

Thater concludes her story of this remarkable project: "I had no idea I was going to do that in the installation. I found the thing that I didn't expect to creep in. In this case, it came from a very simple way to fold space or to make people think of folded space." And as she discovers space folding around the last male northern rhino, she is sparked to move with that new knowing and explore it further in her next work. "It became the starting point for the next piece, the thing I realized after making the work. The thing that is there that I never plan to be there, that appears and, in turn, produces a new idea in the making."

SCREENPLAYS AND ADAPTATION

Talking with the creators of original or adapted screenplays adds another element to our understanding of what it means to enter uncertainty. Like Thater with her Sudan project, screenwriters are often required to work within certain specific structures from the very earliest stage of a project: the two-hour film framework, the limitations inherent in scene and plot construction, actor availability, and so on. I ask screenwriter and novelist Ross LaManna to articulate the difference, for him, between the two genres in which he engages.

"Screenwriting in many ways is easier than novel writing because infinite possibilities have been taken away from you," he explains. "You have to create within the structure. And so a lot of things are off the table, and that's actually a good thing because as long as you know that it has to be one hundred twenty pages, and that there needs to be, more or less, a three-act structure, and that the hero has to do this, and that the villain has to do that—then, you can do whatever you want within that and there's great satisfaction in knowing that you created something new within that framework."

Make to know happens for LaManna in the spaces between the markers of his structure. His process differs from a full-blown entrance into a world of uncertainty, at least practically, but the fundamental exploration/discovery cycle still happens for him as he writes in these interstitial spaces. Countering the filmmaking conventions that often rely heavily on structure, Jean-Luc Godard famously quipped that a film needs "a beginning, a middle, and an end, but not necessarily in that order."

As a result of this conversation with LaManna, I became curious about the process of adaptation in film, when a writer begins with the already established world of a novel or play. Does this meaningfully change the ways in which, say, screenwriters might think about entering into a place of uncertainty, about outlines and conventional structures? With an already existing text, one might expect a screenwriter to think very differently from a novelist or a poet.

In *Signs and Meaning in the Cinema*, film theorist Peter Wollen articulates a point regarding film directing and the independence of the adapter: "The director does not subordinate himself to another author;

his source is only a pretext, which provides catalysts, scenes which fuse with his own preoccupations to produce a radically new work."[19] To translate Wollen's point for our purposes, the adapter (in this case the screenwriter/director) is able to use the first text as a point of entry into the creative process. It is conceivable, therefore, that in producing a recreated text through adaptation, the make-to-know experience can be fully operative, without preconceived vision and with an entry into the unknown.

I'm not suggesting that this is always the case. What I am proposing, however, is the possibility that even in adaptation—a process that at first glance seems to be the polar opposite to entering the unknown—the fundamental make-to-know experience can be essentially the same. The comparison that comes to mind is that of a jazz musician riffing off a version of a melody through improvisation. That form of performance is a kind of live adaptation with variations on melody and theme. Where the musician goes in improvisation is unpredictable. To put it in Wollen's language, the first melody is a "catalyst" that the musician uses, live, to produce a new work. Adaptation is not about slavish copying. It is not about fidelity to an original. It is, in many ways, about making something one's own and, in that making, rendering a new layer of knowing.

A wonderful and well-known example of translating a book to film, where the knowing only comes from the making, is Charlie Kaufman's 2003 film *Adaptation*. "Catalyzed" by Susan Orlean's book *The Orchid Thief*, Kaufman's film, directed by Spike Jonze, provides a convincing case for written adaptation as an inherently revelatory process of making.

In his book *Adaptation: The Shooting Script*, writer and filmmaker Rob Feld interviews Kaufman and Jonze about their collaborations. He asks them about the screenwriter's point of entry into the process. Kaufman replies: "It depends. Sometimes it's an event, sometimes it's more thematic. In this case [*Adaptation*] it was a book....I like to feel free. I don't want to know too much when I start. I want to be free to go with it where it takes me."[20]

Kaufman engages with the writing, in his words, "to surprise himself." He speaks of "fortuitous accidents," of things that surface in a cosmology through the writing itself. "It's a bit scary and fun for that reason because I don't know how it's going to end. It helps me keep going." He goes on to describe the process of discovering structure as he creates and as he goes through the necessary process of revision and shaping that follows his early drafts.

In the specific case of adapting *The Orchid Thief*, Kaufman reaffirms that he really had no particular vision for the screenplay. He was simply intrigued with a book "about flowers—there was very little drama in it." But intrigue, for him, fairly rapidly turned to burning frustration, and he wanted to quit. He states in the interview, and actually echoed the sentiment in a scene in the movie, that he might have dropped the project entirely had the studio not already "paid me a certain amount of money to proceed."

Necessity can be a critical element of creativity, a reality that compels artists to explore worlds that seem alien, frightening, or seemingly uninspired. My interest is not so much in what creates that necessity (money, deadlines, a first rehearsal, a school assignment, or tying oneself to the chair), but in how it compels the artist to enter a world that is unknown, a point of entry in its own right. Perhaps waiting around for a vision to manifest is a product of the same reluctance expressed by Kaufman; and perhaps we have for too long mistaken predetermined vision, seeing the angel in the stone, for a magic key that gives access to an otherwise mysterious world. Such thinking leads to a limited, if not misguided, understanding of the creative process. We need to brave possibility, and sometimes we need the catalyst of necessity to force our entry.

What, then, happened to Kaufman during the process of adapting Orlean's book? As Rob Feld tells it:

> ...the book describes Orlean's experience with a Florida man, John Laroche, who had been arrested for poaching rare orchids from preservation swamplands....Kaufman soon found himself with a dilemma: How the hell does one dramatize a flower? The advance check had been cashed though, and a script was expected from him. After numerous false starts, Kaufman's solution was to

insert into Orlean's true story a fictionalized character named Charlie Kaufman, who happens to be a screenwriter hired to adapt *The Orchid Thief*.[21]

Kaufman found his way to this self-referential moment through multiple "false starts" (read revelatory process) of writing. He was creating/making his way to a solution, not envisioning it. And so the film's name, *Adaptation*, takes on its appropriate meaning, with brilliant echoes of make to know. The personalized plot of the screenplay and its title illustrate that the creation and the thing created have a simultaneity which reflects both process and content in rich relationship. "*Adaptation* is about a writer who becomes fixated on the woman whose experience he's trying to represent in his writing," Rob Feld tells us.[22] It's a perfect illustration of make to know. And the story is still about a flower.

The oscillation of book and screenplay, of first and second texts, of two worlds in dynamic, of adaptation itself, is itself central to the experience of the film. As Kaufman reflects, "Take real people, and take the person who really wrote it, and make them characters, and have the experience of watching them write it *be* the experience that the moviegoer has. So you're constantly being taken out of the movie. Even though you're watching the movie as a story that places a story, there is this constant nagging thing that's, 'Is this real, is this not real?' I really like that."

These comments offer yet another important insight into make to know. Just as the real and the fictional form a central dynamic of the film, so too do making and knowing for the artist. The blurred lines between reality and fiction parallel exactly how artists speak of the fusing of discovery in the process of creating. To paraphrase Kaufman's comments for writers: "Take the writer and make him/her both subject and creator of the thing being written and let the experience of writing *be* the experience of knowing the thing written. There is a constant nagging, 'is this making or knowing?'" When process and product become one, make to know is in balance. And the making and the object made are represented by the same word: "adaptation." Just like "improvisation." If I had to offer an example of watching make to know in action, I could offer nothing more illustrative than the film *Adaptation*.

When I ask filmmaker Zack Snyder about the process of adaptation, he is very direct about the first text: "I'm not trying to reinvent [the book] as best I can. I'm trying to get at the parts that I think are amazing...the things I care about." At the time of our conversation, he is in the middle of working on an adaptation of Ayn Rand's 1943 novel *The Fountainhead*, previously made into a 1949 film starring Gary Cooper. Rand herself wrote the adaptation for the 1949 movie, and a rough draft of her screenplay is central to Snyder's process. "I found [Rand's] rough draft in the archives. Warner archives. Un-photocopied, rough draft, 380 pages. And that's what I've used a lot as a spine." His adaptation is for a ten-part television miniseries.

As the conversation evolves, I begin to understand what Snyder means by the things he "cares about." Like Kaufman and several others, it has to do with "surprise" and all that strikes him as he finds the "voice" of the piece he is adapting. "I've read the book maybe a dozen times. But as I get into the minutiae of the text in my writing, I keep discovering more....And I think what surprises me about my writing is all about getting to the voice. Can I get the voice, can I feel it? I'm doing a dance with the book, I'm trying to groove with the book. When I change something or when I move something, it moves in the way that it *would* move, you know."

He tells me about an original scene he has added that helps to make sense of certain characters and plot threads. After doing this, when he re-read the script several days later, he had forgotten all about writing that original scene—and at first, he didn't recognize it as his own addition. That to him was the great test: the scene adhered well and didn't stand out. "Maybe that's the right groove. I clearly tricked myself."

Snyder writes to find surprise. Like many artists, he must work at it every day in a rhythm. He might have an outline for an original script or a text he is adapting, but he understands that he uses that simply as a way to enter "a scary place" of not knowing. "And I feel like every artist should probably put themselves there as much as they can."

What is this screenwriter's entry point into this frightening world? "It can be anything. Something I see. It can be a photograph, a painting—or a real moment." What he finds is that he can take that stimulus and explore the "scary place" by following the path opened and made possible. "In a movie, you can string an idea that's captured your imagination—it exists in space and time and it moves. You have to chase it to find out what it wants. That thing that first sparked you forces questions: What is that? Or why? And if it's rich enough it will continue. It makes the sidewalk that you walk on. And it will change, and it will evolve."

Make to know, as I have stressed, is not "winging it." There is a direct link, in fact, between the quality of making, no matter the medium, and the level of skill, experience, education, ethics, and engagement that one brings to the work. But those are elements that serve as scaffolding on which the artist stands in creative activity to enter the unknown and the unimaginable.

Snyder echoes that very notion when we discuss his writing. He finds at some points moments of "flow." "That's what keeps you going," he says. "It's like golf. Like that one good shot." He goes on, "I'm not a big golfer, so I don't know why this just came to me, but there is this amazing notion in a book called *The Little Green Golf Book*. The point the author makes is that you have to be good enough to give luck a chance. I think that's underrated in the creative process." He goes on, "Only by first achieving a level of skill can you get to a place where you can be open to the process. You can respond to surprise, realize the thing, because you know how to do it once it comes. You can realize the greatest idea in the world—but only if you can catch it."

Snyder's screenwriting process does not end with the completion of the script. There is a second level of make to know in his work, a different kind of writing. He turns his scripts into detailed storyboards before a shoot. "Once the script is written, I write the script again in drawings. I start again at the beginning. Page one. I open it and I start drawing. And I draw all the shots in cut sequence. So I'll redraw a close-up if I'm going to cut back to it. It takes me months and months."

He then shows me storyboards from *Watchmen*, beautiful volumes of sketchbooks filled with drawings, ideas for visual effects, occasional photographs that he has found. It is a visual treasure, as detailed and rich as the written text, perhaps more so.

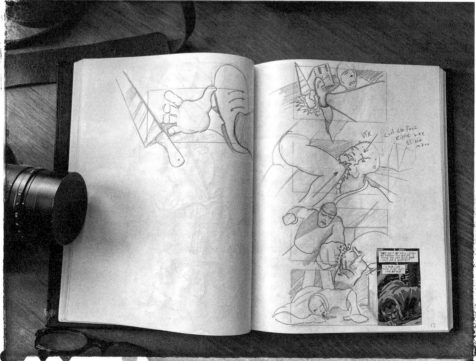

Snyder reflects on drawing and storyboarding as a way to be precise in his writing. He admits that during the shoot there are moments where he needs to be improvisational and where he will be spontaneous in the moment. But his storyboards keep him honest, in a way, and get him deeper into the written script already created. "I find I am always searching for that second layer. And I always like to be conscious of the *why* of it. And I think that when I do the drawings off the script, I build a careful relationship between the words and the images and the shot-planning. *Watchmen* I think is such an important work of literature, I really wanted to be careful with it in the translation. Drawing is all about making sure that the subtext is always working. On the day of the shoot, when the actor is late and you don't have enough time, you can lose that subtext. Storyboarding ensures I get it."

Despite his considerable abilities as a screenwriter, Snyder is fundamentally a visual thinker. "I think that when I draw through it, I'm making. I always say I make the movie for the first time when I draw it." His *drawing* is what allows him to *know* what the movie is about. "It's my illuminated text." These skills, one might also say, give "luck a chance."

Then he offers an interesting digression: "My wife was saying to me the other day: 'Have you ever thought about not writing the script and just drawing the whole thing?' That's interesting to me. I would be interested to see what would happen if I tried it—but I don't think the studio would like it very much."

The detail of his drawings can, on occasion, get him into trouble. He will correct, for example, an actor's movements based on his drawing. "I'll say to them, 'You stand here. See? You stand here, like I drew it.'" Some actors find it difficult, he reflects, "but they get used to it. And sometimes they tell me, no." This same kind of conflict can happen with his production designer as well. "I drew the door's hinges on the other side! You hinged it on the wrong side. The next shot is over there and the door blocks everything." His attention to his illustrations might

Zack Snyder's sketchbook with storyboards
for the movie *Watchmen* (2009).

irritate his production designer, "but the drawings allow me to think at that level of detail."

When I press Snyder on how much he is able to actually improvise during the shoot and deviate from the drawings, he guesses that he probably does change things half the time. "It's the reality of human beings in space and at the table; once you get everyone there, the drawing is fine, but you need to make the thing. And it's only a blueprint. But the blueprint gives me freedom. Without the drawing, I can't organize what needs to be done. I combine the drawing with the reality of what is happening on the set."

REVISION

A work is never completed except by some accident such as weariness, satisfaction, the need to deliver, or death: for, in relation to who or what is making it, it can only be one stage in a series of inner transformations.
—PAUL VALÉRY[23]

Every writer talks about revision. It is a central part of just about any making process and means various things at various times—from starting over to editing to polishing prose, and everything in between. It is interesting to pause for a moment to contemplate what that might mean in the context of make to know. Do writers think about revision as "new vision," "changed vision," or "visioning again"? And if there is not a vision to begin with, how can there exist a "re-vision"? Can we think about revision as a remaking, and therefore a deeper way of knowing?

I return to Tom Stern and his work on *My Vanishing Twin*. You will recall that Stern wrote his way to understanding and knowing his character and that it led to a pivotal moment of discovery, which took place while he was sitting on his bed next to his sleeping wife. The image came to him that he was embarking on a story about a man who is pregnant with his own twin brother. "The next morning, I got up and I sat down to write, and I was focused on this notion. I'm trying not to over-define it or over-name it." As Stern continues to speak, I take particular note of his language—he talks about this pivotal image as a "notion" and as a "central circumstance." But it is still not a vision of the novel. "And all I have are these pages of this guy doing stuff that I wrote in a process of discovery."

"And so how do you get from those pages to this new central circumstance?" I ask.

"I start over from the first page. I probably had forty or fifty pages of character-based stuff then. I just start back from page one and begin moving again. I'm reshaping it with the understanding that we are now heading in this general direction. Layering on a new level, but also adjusting it. Whereas it made sense for the character to react to something in a certain way before, I can now see that he wouldn't react to that thing in the same way because of these new circumstances. Or understanding that the argument I wrote between him and his girlfriend is really about an inability for him to accept the fact that he's pregnant."

Stern discovers through the writing that the preoccupation of his central character is an experience of revulsion toward himself. It begins to color his whole world, and it informs the shape of the scenes. Stern observes the direction of the novel through this process. And as he "writes again" in "revision," another discovery surfaces: his character "is pregnant with his twin brother, *and the twin brother is a genius, with a predilection for business.* That's what has now occurred to me," he explains. "And then that circumstance starts to shape the whole. And I go back to the beginning and start again."

Stern's process, then, is one in which he writes through to discover his character or situation. Either in the writing itself or in a fresh context (sitting on the bed), he comes to a realization. With that realization, he returns to the beginning and adds the new layer. In that process, he discovers yet another element that prompts him to start again, layering on this next piece. The writing of the novel is a continuous process of discovery and revision, of making to know to remaking to know again.

During my interview with Joe Di Prisco, he says: "I can't think of any book I've ever written that I didn't rewrite twenty-five times, maybe more."

This prompts me to ask him a practical question, with Tom Stern very much in mind. "Do you actually complete a whole draft and then go back to the beginning to revise? Or do you write a few pages, revise those, write a few more...?"

"I think both. It's a very fluid process," he reveals. "It's not linear at all. I wake up with an idea or a sentence I wrote that I liked. And then I attack it, stay on it. And then things begin to unravel, like pulling a little stitch of a Persian rug and changing the whole thing."

Di Prisco engages in a revision process of continued discovery and making. He offers an example from his novel *All for Now* that sounds very much like Stern's practice. "You keep finding stuff. With *All for Now*, I didn't realize until I got to the end of the novel what it was. And then I had to go back to figure out all those things that impact the character along the way. I had to ask how it all manages to inform him as he goes through this story that he is telling. It just excited the hell out of me that I found that. It was a lot of work because I had to go back and fill in all the spaces." This is pure make to know, even in the context of a process of revision. Again, we witness an artist articulating that he did not know his work until he got to the end—until he made it. And then he enters into a kind of dialogue with the work, and in that dialogue further making (and further knowing) evolves.

At one point in our conversation, Di Prisco tells me that he has actually realized entirely new characters and invented whole new scenes through the process of revision. And at the end, he concludes: "It might be as simple as this: there is no such thing as revision, there's just rewriting. You just keep writing. It's not so much revising what you've done. It's like seeing it again. Doing it again." To be sure, it is making again.

Aimee Bender characterizes revision as "acute listening" and as an attempt to imagine herself as the reader. The challenge, of course, is that for the writer, who created the material in the first place and is already familiar with it, true "acute listening" is problematic. It requires some level of disruption. Bender tries quite deliberately to "de-familiarize" the material so that she can "access it again." She wants to engage as if she were seeing the writing for the first time.

"How do you get into that—those eyes?"

She employs various strategies. She will print out material instead of reading it on the screen. Or, on occasion, she will follow the advice of Susan Bell, who, in *The Artful Edit*, talks about changing the font of her text as a way to see anew.[24] Whatever Bender's technique, her purpose is to get to a point of optimal clarity, to check blind spots and ego. "Just the usual kill-your-darlings mode," she quips, "where there's a line that I'm attached to for several reasons, and I'm working up the courage to cut it."

Di Prisco says the same thing, almost verbatim. "There's a kind of courage of being a writer, and to have the strength to throw stuff out." The knowing that comes from making can also take the form of subtraction. Revision is a phase of that work.

Bender goes on to say that when she goes back to look at the writing, "either it's working, or it's not working. And if it's working, then the revision I do falls more into the editing mode. And there will be drastic cuts within that, but the central drive is intact. And if it's not working, I won't work on it. I don't really feel like you can make a thing *not* working, work."

"And so then what happens?" I ask.

"It just sits there," she replies. "And maybe someday when I have a little time, I reopen it, and I find that it re-engages me, and then I start the editing process again. Or it will show up in a new form in a new story or novel, but I won't know it because it will feel like a new thing. I found an angle into it, and that means there's a freshness in the language that I didn't have."

"What about the editing itself?"

"It's line by line and filling in places where I think it can develop. I pay attention to rhythm almost more than anything. How is the pacing? How are the beats?" As Bender speaks, her statement about rhythm resonates clearly with my own work. There is indeed a kind of listening, almost musical, that guides revision. It describes well a nuance of making in this phase and how one enters the particular uncertainty that exists when revisiting previously created material.

I asked Bender if she thinks at all about her process of revision as a layering—a new text imaginatively positioned on the one previous to it. "Yeah, there is a building of the sensory world, the memory world, the language, all of that comes in." And then she returns to rhythm and to acute listening to get at how she finds her way in this "layering." "Rhythm feels really important to that because it also may require a kind of de-layering if it feels too cluttered. It's very much this sense of how the reader metabolizes the information. How am I metabolizing it? Do I feel like this is racing by me? Do I feel like I'm bombarded with information of all kinds? How am I processing this as I read it?"

Finally, I explore with her my ideas regarding adaptation—which, as she spoke, I suddenly realized were entirely relevant to the issue of revision. In thinking about adaptation, I discovered that working with a first text is no less a move into uncertainty than writing, say, a novel from scratch. The example of Charlie Kaufman makes it clear that adaptation can be a journey into the unknown, into make to know. Perhaps revision operates on the same principle. You begin with a first text and then create another in revision, and then a third, each time a re-engagement to find again, to discover in the act of making the subsequent text, as you did with the first. Perhaps revision is finding a new point of entry into a world equally uncertain, a different access point than the first.

This comparison seems to resonate with Bender. "I think it's a really neat parallel. And there are many strands that line up. When you're revising, there's something in that first text that's raw, and sort of not quite there yet. And so you are also adapting it by bringing it into being. And with adaptation, you're having to make it raw in order to adapt it, right? Because if you let it be too much of its own thing that's complete, there's no reason to adapt. I think for an adapter, you have to treat the original text like you're revising it."

Many of the writers I've interviewed seem to associate revision with a risk of facing failure. On one level, a writer can feel, while engaged in an early stage of writing, that something substantive and important surfaces; but on further review, it sometimes turns out that the work is not as good as it initially seemed.

Here's Di Prisco again: "I have on my computer unfinished books, things I have started, could be a hundred pages in, that I have lost interest in. That's embarrassing to note, but it's true."

"Why is it embarrassing?" I ask.

"I've invested this effort. How did I fail? I failed the story. I had something and I blew it."

Tom Stern also talks of failure, but from a different angle. "I am always unclear when people say they love writing but don't like editing. To me they are the same. In the beginning, you are editing with nothing. You just need to start somewhere. If I let myself I could, after one sentence, think 'That's not right, let's go back and fix that.' To me the writing is a process of failing, failing, failing forward until hopefully I have something."

And then Stern goes deeper and explains that for him revision, like all making, is never fully complete—and his work will always be a failure in that regard. He will never really be able to say anything fully. Referencing Flannery O'Connor, he suggests that his interest is ultimately in articulating something beyond anything he can do with language. "To that end, the work is hopefully saying more than I'm capable of saying. I don't view what is incomplete in a bad way, but I do view it as a failing. I understand how to strive after something and get a part of the way there, but not get all the way. It never arrives and it can't ever truly arrive. And so it all feels like it's ultimately a failure, because I could always come back and continue to move forward. I never really finish. I simply reach a point where I've gone as far as I'm capable of pushing it."

As Stern speaks, I think of W.H. Auden's well-known paraphrase of Valéry: "A poem is never finished; it is only abandoned." Revision includes, in the end, the moment when making must rest; and that may well be a moment of reckoning with failure or, in the language of this book, with the limitations of knowing.

When is work complete? For Stern, it is when he reaches a point where he simply believes he cannot push any further. For Aimee Bender, on the other hand, her work is finished when she feels she has captured an emotional moment in as complete a way as she can with words. "I feel like I've done everything I can to have a clarity of feeling. And then it is done. I once talked about writing as a kind of terrarium. I'm just trying to capture the live thing. That's all I want. I want to capture something that has life in it...as long as I feel like it has life in it. And then, once I feel that is adequately captured, I do feel done. What else am I supposed to do with it?"

These conversations exploring questions of the complete work remind me of some key reflections by Roland Barthes on writing the novel—reflections that sit beautifully alongside the ideas discussed by the writers and artists I've spoken to. In *The Rustle of Language*, Barthes suggests that the novel is a form of making that produces what he calls "the truth of affects." He shifts attention from product to practice—indeed, to the making itself. "And here I regain, to conclude, a method. I put myself in the position of the subject who *makes* something, and no longer of the subject who speaks *about* something: I am not studying a product, I assume a production....The world no longer comes to me as an object, but as a writing, i.e., a practice: I proceed to another type of knowledge....I venture a hypothesis and I explore, I discover the wealth of what follows from it..."[25]

We enter uncertainty. We make. We practice our creativity in order to enter another type of knowledge. The creative is always in movement, in the making, never complete (more making is always conceivable and possible). Producing simply stops at a point; it comes to a moment of readiness of the writer to share and to create for another a further level of making—the reading itself.

Chapter 3

ENGAGING MATERIALS: SEEKING THE FORMS OF THINGS UNKNOWN

I sometimes begin a drawing with no preconceived problem to solve, with only the desire to use pencil on paper, and make lines, tones and shapes with no conscious aim; but as my mind takes in what is so produced, a point arrives where some idea becomes conscious and crystallizes, and then a control and ordering begin to take place.
—HENRY MOORE[1]

I don't know what I'm doing. And it's the not knowing that makes it interesting.
—PHILIP GLASS[2]

Let us get better at not knowing what we're doing.
—DEAN YOUNG[3]

What do the materials of making reveal? And how does the artist's engagement with materials, broadly defined, open up ways to possibility and discovery?

Tom Stern says that he "moves words around" in order to find direction and meaning; but what about the painter, the installation artist, the theater artist, the musician, or the illustrator? What is "moved around" in their processes of making, and to what end? Artists play with the materials of their given practice to find a way into their work, to feel its dimensions and nuances, and eventually to reach a place of knowing something about it and where it might lead. The texture of the clay, the surface of the canvas, the thickness of the paint, the light of the shot, the space in which a performance takes place—all of these are tangible pathways into uncertainty, portals into what a work might be.

In November 2017, I had the pleasure of spending a day with artist Ann Hamilton at her studio in Columbus, Ohio. Hamilton is one of a very few people who helped me conceptualize the make-to-know process in the first place, and she did this through her installation work, her writing, and various interviews and readings. She is a kindred spirit when it comes to thinking about creativity, and I have learned a great deal from her and from her meditations on the subject. Her exquisite essay "Making Not Knowing," adapted from her 2005 commencement address at the School of the Art Institute of Chicago, is a case in point. Her writing is deeply relevant, as is her description of the making/knowing relationship: "One doesn't arrive...by necessarily knowing where one is going. In every work of art, something appears that does not previously exist."[4]

In a conversation with Krista Tippett for the *On Being* podcast (November 19, 2015), Hamilton further clarifies her earlier reflections: "When you're making something, you don't know what it is for a really long time. So, you have to kind of cultivate the space around you, where you can trust the thing that you can't name.... And, if you feel a little bit insecure, or somebody questions you, or you need to know what it is, then what happens is you give that thing that you're trying to listen to away, and so how do you...cultivate a space that allows you to dwell in that—not knowing...?"[5]

In a very specific way, for Hamilton, cultivating a space of not knowing is a preparation and, importantly, a kind of dialogue with the material elements of her work. She is interested in what a discipline of "not knowing" might yield, how it opens mind and heart; it is a deliberate act (and a *making*) that can produce, for her, a moment of "recognition." It is a courageous journey to creative possibility: "Not knowing isn't ignorance. (Fear springs from ignorance.) Not knowing is a permissive and rigorous willingness to trust, leaving knowing in suspension, trusting in possibility without result, regarding as possible all manner of response....Our task is the practice of recognizing."

I ask Hamilton directly if "recognition" means the same to her as "surprise," a word that has surfaced frequently in my conversations with various writers about this topic. The two concepts are not the same, she asserts with some conviction. "The goal, I think, is to find a process that is unselfconscious," she tells me, "so that you lose your sense of intention in order to become responsive." I am struck by her words; there is beauty, I feel, in the promise of an "unselfconscious" state of making, an attitude of responsiveness in order to "make" recognition possible.

"You know, there's a hunch in what you started, right?" she elaborates. "But it's not something you can execute or realize; you can only open the path. Through the making, one comes to recognize the question. And then you are doing what you need to do, and it will lead you to the next thing, whatever that is, in time."

I pose to artist and designer Rebeca Méndez the same question about whether, for her, the making experience leads to surprise or recognition. She answers without hesitation (and with a passion equal to Hamilton's) that her process is about a "beautiful recognition." And, again like Hamilton, she is deliberate in her work in this regard. Méndez uses the word "unlearn" as she discusses her process.

"I have found that my understanding of things in my state of limited knowledge is an obstacle whenever I want to be creative. When I really want to engage with something (almost mate with an idea or subject matter), I need to enter with complete curiosity the beginner's mind. If I presume to know, I impose my limits on the subject matter. It's the beginner's mind I seek, where I approach the material like a child, with wonder and curiosity. It is then that I begin to befriend the subject matter."

"Do you see that beginner's mind as a necessary preparation to get to the point of recognizing?"

"I do. Otherwise, I'm really just imposing something if I feel I know. There's something completely destructive about thinking that one knows all the time. Reflecting now, on the subject matter now, and on my location now, will bring a completely different truth than what I might have had in my understanding, say, ten years ago. I love when [French philosopher Gilles] Deleuze says that every truth depends on certain coordinates, required elements, a time and a place. I think for me this idea of not knowing, unlearning, allows me to perceive. I am a raider of perception. But I have to be open and receptive to *what is*, and not impose old filters of understanding."

"But why is it recognition to you?"

"You need to remember what life is," she insists. "We are as humans incredibly receptive. Our whole life is receiving, receiving, receiving, and it is only our limited ego mind and role definitions that keeps us from actually exploring what we have gathered throughout our entire lives....Yes, it is recognition."

Surprise and recognition: both are critical elements of the make-to-know process and represent different kinds of markers in the space of creative uncertainty. "Surprise" suggests a sudden feeling of wonder and astonishment at the unforeseen. The word has an etymological connection to the French *surprendre*, from *sur-* (over) and *prendre* (to take), as well as to the Latin *superprehendre* from *prendere*, contracted from *prehendre*, to grasp or seize. We are clutched and "overtaken" in surprise.

When we "recognize," we have a sense of identifying something previously seen, heard, known—or the echo of same. The concept is distinctly different, then, from the unlooked-for quality connoted by "surprise." One meaning of the noun "recognition" is "acceptance," an aspect of the term that illuminates yet another element of make to know. One "accepts" what the process of making offers. Recognition is linguistically related to "knowing again," "recalling to mind," "acknowledging," "identifying" (Old French *reconoistre*). The Latin etymology, however, offers a nuanced but important difference: *recognoscere*, from *re-* (again) and *cognoscere* (to get to know). With recognition, we have an opportunity "to get to know again," to recall.

Tom Stern was "surprised," I think, that his book turned out to be about a man who was pregnant with his brother. He wrote those many pages so that he might find the surprise; once found, the surprise did "overtake" the whole. Ann Hamilton, on the other hand, develops a "practice of responsiveness" that has everything to do with engaging with materials, confronting space, touching, shaping, seeing again. She gives me an example from her celebrated installation *the event of a thread*, exhibited at the Park Avenue Armory in New York City in 2012.

"I remember when we were working on the Armory project and Marty, this wonderful theater guy and engineer who was helping me, drove in through the loading dock door, which is at the end of the drill hall, you know, the trucks come in and out to load everything. And I

Ann Hamilton, *the event of a thread*. Commissioned by Park Avenue Armory, New York, December 5, 2012–January 6, 2013.

happened to be at the opposite end, just walking through the doors from the inside. And it was the first time I had that view through to Lexington Avenue. And we were within two weeks of opening; we were scrambling. And at that moment I thought, 'oh, so that's what we need.' I knew there were some important elements at the end of the space over there. I had a sense that they were right, but things weren't in the proper relation yet, and the minute he drove through I could see that I needed the spine of light. It's about recognition." She then offers a clever twist of language: "It's the part of the process about how you come to know the thing that you don't know that you know." It is finding cognition in recognition.

THE MATERIAL OF SPACE

Ann Hamilton engages with space the way a painter engages with the canvas, a sculptor with wire, a typographer with letterform. The space she develops is a fundamental "material" element of her work. "I think a lot about how I structure space," she tells me, offering examples of her passion for particular places, from an unusual auditorium at the University of Chicago to a little opera theater in China. She talks about "feeling" the space. She needs to stand in it to find its resonance. There's nothing theoretical about it. "I need to put the space in play; I have to walk a place into my body—the only way I know how to begin is to walk it, just walk it. What is the space asking? You need to be there every day, all day long, changing and tweaking and responding all the way through—because that's how you know it, by doing it."

Hamilton enters a space already existing, a cosmology not initially of her making, but one that nonetheless opens the possibility of recognition through something she creates or places within it. She is very deliberate in her language: "How do you make a structure to move within? That for me is the space...You put a piece of cloth on the floor. And then you reflect, 'What are all the ways this could be? Is it paper? Is it a square? Is it white?' And you realize, when you ask yourself all these really simple, dumb questions, that you know you actually don't know." Her work is playful, even in its smallest details. "No, it's not like that. No, it's like this. With every small thing, you reflect on what it can be. And somehow that small piece will have consequence. And every time you make a decision, you need to be conscious that you have a lot of choices, that you're not assuming it has to be something. You're not even aware of your assumptions half the time. You just need to be in a responsive place."

As I listen to Hamilton talk about defining space through placing a piece of cloth on the floor, my own experience of working in the theater comes to mind. When objects or people enter space, a moment of theater can ensue. Hamilton's work, in many respects, has always struck me as theatrical, something she herself confirms in our conversation. The particular example of the piece of cloth, I tell her, reminds me of the work of British director Peter Brook and his concept of "the empty space," itself a notion of uncertainty that yields theatrical possibility. In the 1960s, Brook wrote, "I can take any empty space and call it a bare stage. A man walks across this empty space whilst someone else is watching him, and this is all that is needed for an act of theatre to be engaged."[6] This concept is entirely relevant, not only to the idea of make to know and what might come from what is uncertain and "empty" (or unknown), but to Hamilton's notion of preparing the material of space, "cultivating it," in her words, for some discovery, for a recognition.

The connection of Brook and Hamilton and their engagement with the material of space is instructive and warrants deeper analysis. Her act of placing a cloth in a space to set a process in motion echoes a story told by John Heilpern in his book *The Conference of the Birds*, about the journey of Peter Brook and his acting troupe in the 1970s traveling through the Saharan desert and the Nigerian bush. The troupe performed in various places and to various audiences. They created spaces in which to work, usually by ritualistically rolling out a carpet ("placing a cloth") as the entry into a place of performance, or by creating a circular ring in the desert sand for improvisation. The point was all about making to know, about engaging the material potential of space, about improvisation.

One particularly interesting example of this cultivated space of discovery during the Africa trip is evident in Heilpern's sketch called "The Shoe Show":

A pair of shoes—boots belonging to an actor—are placed in the center of a circle. They are magic shoes, capable of transforming kings into slaves, the old into the young, or a one-legged man into a two-legged man.[7]

A piece of cloth on the floor; shoes placed in a circle in the desert sand—these are points of entry into unknown worlds. They are an activation of space, the beginning of a work of theater, an improvisation, an installation, a kind of magic; they lead ultimately to "recognizing" what that circle, that defined space, might contain, the story it might yield. Brook wanted to explore something essential about performance in a search for what he called "the immediate theatre." Hamilton, likewise, explores possibilities of "a responsive place." "Questions generate questions," she suggests. "That's all you have."[8]

Peter Brook (center) improvising performances during a trip to Africa in 1973 with an international troupe of actors including Helen Mirren (right) © Mary Ellen Mark.

THE MATERIAL OF TIME

I am an admirer of the work of Los Angeles-based installation artist Edgar Arceneaux and the penetrating cultural and historical questions he raises. His process of making is about engaging the temporal in a manner reminiscent of Ann Hamilton's engagement with the spatial; he works with the fabric of time as she does with space. "Part of the reason I am interested in history," he tells me, "the way in which it echoes itself through time, is because, as I am making, it allows me to dislodge certain things in the subconscious, it gives physical language to manifest itself in the present."

Arceneaux's project *Until, Until, Until...*, which I saw in 2017, is at once an installation, a film project, and, at times, a theatrical presentation. The piece is centered around a re-enactment of actor Ben Vereen's profoundly misinterpreted "blackface" performance at Ronald Reagan's 1981 inaugural gala.[9]

The final section of Vereen's performance at the gala, which expressed the actor's critique of the history of the minstrel show, was cut and never televised. This meant that the television audience viewed only the "set-up" performed by Vereen in blackface—with absolutely no critical context. It came off as a grotesque capitulation (or worse) by an African American artist. Vereen was deeply embarrassed and the African American community understandably enraged.

Until, Until, Until... and Arceneaux's work generally interests me on many levels, but particularly for its interrogation of temporal experience in relation to current perception. "You start to see yourself as being part of a larger continuum," Arceneaux tells me, "and then there are different ways in which you move with that realization within a project."

In the case of *Until, Until, Until...*, Arceneaux engages layers of time quite deliberately. First, a contemporary viewer, in real time, observes footage of Ben Vereen's performance. At strategic moments, that same viewer sees shots of the 1981 televised audience watching Vereen who, in full blackface, is offering an homage to the early 20th-century vaudeville performer Bert Williams. Echoes of time—the present, 1981, the age of vaudeville and blackface. Arceneaux creates temporal contours in precise choreography.

Edgar Arceneaux, "Looking at Ben, Looking at Ben," 2015–20.
Photo from the performance project *Until, Until, Until...*

The multiple temporal layers of spectator viewing that are central to Arceneaux's piece evolved through the making, but his process of getting there, his moment of recognition, came about as one of those "happy accidents" which, as we have seen, are part of a continuum of creative engagement: shower moments, driving moments, dreams. They are part of a readiness to know, not unlike Ann Hamilton's "recognizing" the necessity of a spine of light in a space through the seemingly random opening of a loading dock door.

Arceneaux tells me the story of his happy accident. "We were still working on the show and on the script. I don't think we had actually started our first set of rehearsals. But I was invited to Long Beach Community College to do a presentation. And toward the end, I told them I was working on this piece. I didn't know how it was going to turn out. I was feeling pretty anxious. And then I said to them spontaneously,

'I actually have the full ten-minute Vereen performance. Would you like to watch it?'

"I put it on for them, and it was the first time I had the experience of watching it with a big group. And I could sit there watching them watching it. And I saw this woman sitting next to me crying, and it dawned on me only at that moment that the show was about the audiences, about being seen and about who is looking. I drove home with this realization. I sat in my driveway and sketched it all out. It's about the audience—it's about the audience. And only through that experience did I realize that I had to figure out how to transition the audience from being a viewer to being a participant." In the end, audiences layered in time gave the piece meaning, something that emerged only in the making.

In his *Watts House Project*, an artist-driven neighborhood redevelopment enterprise in South Los Angeles that Arceneaux tells me was really "an art piece masquerading as a community project" and "an installation on a larger level of community development," the artist

Edgar Arceneaux, *Watts House Project*: home across the street from Watts Towers receives a floral makeover from Project workers in 2008.

Watts House Project launch event.

similarly entered his work through a question about time. "If you're working in neighborhood development in a historically marginalized community like Watts, you have to ask, 'why does this neighborhood look the way it does when you can drive ten minutes in another direction and, in a very similar neighborhood, find all these resources? What is it that created these conditions?' And then you think about the echo of time, and recognize that the conditions in which you're existing currently were produced by decisions that were made fifty years ago." But what stimulated those questions about time came about through the making, and it concerned specifically Arceneaux's encounter of and connection to the famous Watts Towers that stand across the street from his venture. Built over the course of thirty-three years by the Italian immigrant Simon Rodia (in his backyard), the towers are icons of a neighborhood, structures that have proclaimed a region, monumental edifices of temporal resonance. In Arceneaux's words, "Rodia built what, in my opinion, is one of the most important sculptural works in the 20th century."

Arceneaux's association with the towers set a process in motion, and the structures ultimately functioned as a kind of temporal set for his drama of change and redevelopment. As architect Frank Gehry points out during our interview (a conversation I will return to in Chapter 4), the making process, as an engagement with the material of time, involves deep and important dialogues with buildings and structures of the past. Those dialogues inspire new layers of meaning as work evolves around them. Make to know is also a conversation.

"When you're making something," Arceneaux explains, "you're really in the creative space when you're having a conversation with the thing in relationship to you and to other things. It's telling you what it wants to be. Sometimes, that could be an absolute defiance of what

Watts Towers by Simon Rodia. Located in the community of Watts in South Central Los Angeles, the steel towers were designed and built singlehandedly by Rodia from 1921 to 1954. He covered the surfaces of the structure with colorful mosaics of found items.

you wanted. Does it want to be full of contrast? Does it want to have levels of transparency? Should there be staccato? Should there be great variances in scale? Should things be broken up and scattered or should they be one sequential experience? When you start to think about it in that way, it frees you up to what it can be—the material manifestation emerges only from that process. And from that activity, it will start to take on some geometry. It will take on some shape."

THE MATERIALS OF PAINTING
Through handling materials in practice,
a form of tacit knowledge arises.
—NITHIKUL NIMKULRAT[10]

Often the materials or processes speak back to the
designer in a way where there is a mutual discovery.
—ROSANNE SOMERSON[11]

Ann Hamilton's engagement with space and Edgar Arceneaux's with time offer striking comparisons with painters and how they think about the materials with which they work. When I interview the artist Stephen Beal, for example, he echoes Arceneaux's language of making as conversation, telling me: "The whole concept everybody talks about regarding iterating and failing is, for me, very much just a dialogue with the material—and you can't get that without making something." He suggests that employing material is exactly what gives him entry into the uncertainties of his paintings. "It's not about an idea; it is part of having a sensitivity or relationship with the material." He thrives on that immediate connection. "The material has characteristics that are right there and have to be engaged. For me, the process of making is about that engagement, whether I'm working with wood or paintings. Everything about my work is significant in this way; making the stretcher bars and preparing the canvases or the linen are all part of it."

He points to some of the paintings on his studio wall. "These paintings all have a unique quality in the linen and the weave. I am hyper-aware of the characteristics of the material I use. I've done a whole series of

Stephen Beal in his studio. "The material has characteristics that are right there and have to be engaged. For me the process of making is about that engagement..."

paintings with just dots. It's a structure to start investigating paint on material."

Illustrator Ann Field, in a conversation I will return to later, talks about material encounter in a similar way: "I love all materials and respond to the visceral qualities, whatever they are. Tactility. I have to feel that pressure of the brush, or the chalk, or stick, or ink, and I have to hear sounds. I have to be smelling it. I have to."

Beal references the artist Agnes Martin, who, he tells me, would draw lines across six-foot canvases with a twelve-inch ruler. "She would just go twelve inches at a time, and there was something about the lead of her pencil meeting the weave of the canvas that gave the line its quality. Even at a basic level, you have to understand the ways in which the lead/weave engagement was critical to how she thought about those paintings." Beal's point about Martin sheds light on make to know. The artist, together with the materials—the lead, the weave, the canvas, the short ruler—are the elements of a making that is in motion and fluid; in time, the elements unite to form the thing made. It is a beautiful alliance of human being and material that is the driving energy of the work. And it is discovery, a kind of knowing that only this process of making might reveal.

Beal talks about how his relationship with materials also fundamentally changes his sense of time and space. For him, the human/material dynamic takes over as the dominant creative context and is all-encompassing. "Making things changes my sense of time. I am in a different relationship with my body, physically doing something. Making a painting demands a specific kind of attention, the attention of viewing, which slows down time, changes time and the perception of it." It also changes his sense of space. "Paintings are picture playing. I'm constantly changing my perception of space in them. And that transformative experience is central. And it's all about how I change material and how the space in the painting changes as a result."

Beal "walks the space" of his work (to use Ann Hamilton's language) in order to keep discovery active. "The interaction with the painting doesn't stop," he says. "I put it aside at some point and think it's enough and perhaps the process has stopped. But three days later—or a week later, or three months later—I go back and realize it's in process. I do something with the material in the painting. I discover something. I might even think I am done. But there's a morning after." Beal re-enters the space of the work to engage the material again. "It has everything to do with my reaction to the physical thing. I can't just imagine how to fix something in a painting by thinking that 'I'm going to put a little pink slash here and it's going to make this green look perfect.' I can't know until I make it, until I actually do it and have a reaction. That's the iterative process of making."

Alexa Meade is a Los Angeles artist whose work lends an interesting perspective on the issue of material encounter and discovery—she paints her portraits physically on the bodies of her subjects and all that surrounds them. "Everything," she explains in a 2013 TED talk, "the person, the clothes, chairs, wall, gets covered in a mask of paint that mimics what is directly below it, and in this way, I am able to take a three-dimensional scene and make it look like a two-dimensional painting."[12]

Meade tells the story of her fascination with shadows and her desire to play with paint and light. That desire eventually led her to experiment with actually painting the body of a friend. She speaks of a very specific "vision" about what that act of painting another person might yield, but that vision led to something very different in the making, in her engagement of the material of paint and the human body. As with Beal, space changed, and she realized an unintended transformation into a two-dimensional world. "Something kept on flickering before my eyes. I wasn't quite sure what I was looking at. And then when I took that moment to take a step back—magic. I had turned my friend into a painting. I couldn't have foreseen that when I wanted to paint a shadow, I would pull out this whole other dimension..."

Alexa Meade, *A Proposal—We Cross the Street*. Paint on the human body led Meade to discover an unintended transformation into a two-dimensional world.

93

Alexa Meade, *Hesitate BTS*, a collaboration between Alexa Meade and Sheila Vand, 2012.

Meade's experimentation with material was quite deliberate and represented a courageous effort to enter a world unknown to her regarding space and light. "I didn't want to teach myself how to paint by copying the old masters or stretching a canvas and practicing over and over again on that surface." Her early experiments included painting on fried food, fruit, and toast. But painting on people became the important activity. She even ended up collaborating with actress and performance artist Sheila Vand, painting her in a pool filled with milk, with all the unusual and unexpected images that came as a result. Her process of making, inextricably tied to an engagement with uncommon and strange materials, revealed a compelling illusion of dimension she could never have envisioned.

GETTING UNSTUCK

Inspiration is for amateurs. The rest of us just
show up and get to work.
—CHUCK CLOSE[13]

For the painter Tom Knechtel, discovery comes via pathways rich in their unpredictability. He cites Lewis Carroll, and echoes as he does Ann Hamilton's admonition to lose intention as a way of moving forward. "My favorite metaphor for the unexpected is in *Through the Looking-Glass*," he tells me excitedly. "After Alice arrives in the looking glass, she sees this beautiful garden outside the house. She tries to walk toward the garden, but the path keeps twisting itself and, inadvertently, the more she takes the obvious path, the more she moves away from where she wants to go. Finally, she gives up. She walks away from the garden and, by doing so, walks into the heart of it."

Knechtel then recalls an anecdote about Chuck Close that echoes Alice's experience. In the documentary *Chuck Close: A Portrait in Progress*, Close discusses an important turning point in his career. As a young artist he was in awe of Willem de Kooning and, as he puts it, "painted more de Koonings than de Kooning."[14] But at a certain point he knew he had to break free and find his own way. So he set himself the task of creating a painting that was diametrically opposed to everything he had emulated from de Kooning: a monumental black-and-white photo-realist image of a naked woman. That radical departure allowed him to find his own language and launched him into his massive photorealist paintings of heads. Close walked away to find the garden.

Reflecting on his own career, Knechtel reveals that, more often than not, finding his way to the "garden" of his work is about overcoming something that frightens or embarrasses him. And it is the very reluctance associated with those feelings, to move in an opposing direction (like Alice), that he identifies as essential to breaking through to a new level. "I walk into the middle of something that I would've never walked into otherwise, and there it is. That's what I was looking for."

The idea of entering something frightening or embarrassing, confronting directly the source of one's anxiety, can be an enormously important element of make to know, something an artist might demonstrate in different phases of a given work or an entire career. This courageous act, moreover, is especially significant when encountering the ruts into which creative people inevitably fall. Knechtel himself talks about how, at one point in his career, he needed to confront his own habits of making and the perils of operating too long in familiar territory. But what is most pertinent here is that he had to *make* to get out of his rut, to get unstuck. Knechtel reflects on the problem: "The process of figuring out how to surprise yourself becomes difficult when you are encumbered with your own languages that have built up. You just keep repeating it all, even without realizing it. It is like, you know, the old Woody Allen line about a relationship—'It's a shark, it has to constantly move forward or it dies.'"

"Habit is a great deadener," reflects Vladimir, a character in Samuel Beckett's *Waiting for Godot*. It is a sentiment familiar to many creative people. Tom Knechtel's experience, however, illustrates how a process of making to know can help one move beyond the habitual—and its deadening consequences—and emerge as deeply relevant to the creative shape of our lives. This is Knechtel's story.

"Imagination had emptied out. I had to find something else," he tells me. He worked for close to two years, trying to find new territory. But he had mixed results. In retrospect, he realized that in this direct attempt to reach something new, he was simply reframing the language in which he worked, but not ultimately what the language was addressing. Like Alice, he was seemingly heading for the garden but, in the process, moving farther away. "I would do a whole series of paintings using a technique I had never used on a material I had never explored. The trouble was, it was still wrestlers and ball gowns and animals on their hind legs talking. And allegorical symbols. Same stuff I had done for years."

The turning point came in an intriguing way. He saw, quite serendipitously at Stanford University's Cantor Arts Center, a small drypoint print by the early 20th-century German artist Lovis Corinth. It was this that sparked the change. "I've never been interested in Corinth, because his work seemed very academic to me. But there was this little drypoint at the museum that shows him looking at a mirror and drawing himself, refusing to look down at what he was doing. The result is a face that looked like it was collapsing under psychic pressure. It was like the features would start moving around."

Knechtel had never created anything like that. "I've never worked from life. I hate it." It frightened him, he reveals, and it was contrary to everything about his artistic practice. "It's a territory that I've always stayed away from. I believed that painting from life came with a certain kind of assumed moral weight—like it was supposed to be better somehow than the painting from a photograph. I just didn't believe that." But what made him anxious was precisely the terrain of an unknown world that he needed

Lovis Corinth, *Self-portrait*, 1924. Drypoint print. Iris & B. Gerald Cantor Center for Visual Arts at Stanford University; Gift of John Flather and Jacqueline Roose.

to explore. And so, after taking twisted paths that ultimately kept him away from the place he was hoping to reach, he went into the very world that had for so long been the object of his resistance. "It was clearly a direction I needed to follow."

The process, as expected, was sometimes difficult, but sometimes it was enthralling. He persevered, creating work that, to him, was uneven at best. "I look back at a show I did about a year later. There were two large paintings. One painting is fine. The other I now see as disastrous because I fell back into some of my old habits, even though I didn't recognize it at the time." Ultimately, however, this period of making, of entering a space of anxiety spurred on by that chance encounter with the Corinth drypoint, transformed his work and sent him in a rich and important direction.

There are a variety of other ways, of course, to get unstuck. Beyond the critical moment of catching sight of the Corinth drypoint, Knechtel echoes almost verbatim the words of Edgar Arceneaux, Stephen Beal, and Diana Thater—to get to new places, he must enter into conversation with the objects of his creation. "It is most exciting when the object I make can ask me questions and help me to understand something else in my thinking." Knechtel engages with his work, and with the thinking and knowing that emerges from it: "The work talks back to me," he asserts. "I look at the work and recognize a certain line of thought that I've never articulated myself, that I find with various pieces of work in dialogue with one another." And that conversation, intriguingly, is the means through which he persists in the creative process. "When a work of art is talking back to me, it is most interesting when it says something that I don't quite understand how to process. The only thing I can do is make another work of art as a way of thinking about the thing I don't fully understand. It's like that wonderful quote from the writer Bernard Cooper. He has this phrase he uses sometimes when he encounters something alien. He says, 'I think I don't know what to eat with it.' For me," Knechtel continues, "that inarticulate state is highly productive and a great way to go into the next drawing. It's wonderful to give enough power over to a work of art so that it can actually stand up on its hind legs and say something back to you that you didn't expect; it can unnerve you or challenge your idea of what you thought you were trying to do."

Getting unstuck can also be a simple making process of repetition and rehearsal. The graphic journalist and illustrator Wendy MacNaughton tells me about how she moves out of stagnant places by going to a café to draw coffee cups. "It's a physical thing. Just to get the motor going. I get my hands moving. I draw a coffee cup and then I draw the profile of somebody who was sitting at a table and then I draw the barista behind the bar. And then the next thing I know, my hand is flowing; it's not stuck anymore in my head. It just starts going. Ideas come, they flow. But if I were to sit there and stare at a wall and try to come up with an idea, I might as well just tear my hair out. It's not going to work. It's through the doing."

MacNaughton sums up what make to know means for her: "Drawing is experiential. If I drew from my imagination, it would be a completely different practice. I draw from life. If I'm not sitting amidst life and taking notes with my hand (which means drawing), then I would have nothing." And yet she confesses to repeated experiences, despite her track record, of feeling stuck. And the only solution is to make, to go to cafés to draw coffee cups or simply to force herself into the world. "I get up and I go into the street, and I draw. For me going out and being there allows things to happen that I could never have imagined. Whether it be sitting down and drawing, keeping the hand going to see what comes of it, or going out and talking to people, drawing them, or turning right instead of left. Whatever it is, I have to go for it—and the most unexpected, beautiful things happen."

Wendy MacNaughton, *Office Hours.*

"A SATELLITE FLOATING AROUND"

Artist and illustrator Esther Pearl Watson compares her creative process to the way she lives her life, as a continuous project of becoming unstuck. "I would just jump into the unknown and go for something. For example, at one point I uprooted and moved to New York City just to try it. I was naïve in one way but just thought I would try to make a go of it. My creativity is similar. I don't want to stay within any boundaries, or with what is comfortable. I want to expand boundaries and disrupt the expected."

Watson compares her process in both life and work with dadaist experiments "where you take an image, cut it up, throw it on the floor and then make something of the chaos that has landed. There's a system to it, but it allows for confusion and failure and all this other stuff to happen." She and I grapple together to understand the nature of what that "system" might be: an organizing principle, a frame, a structure of some kind? We come up with the idea of a "constellation." From that, Watson takes off with many wonderful metaphors of her movement through this constellation of things. "I'm just a little satellite floating around, getting knocked off course *or trying to knock myself off course,*" she says, reminding me again of Alice. "I dodge meteors and debris, always interested in what's pulling me or where I might land. Just traveling through." But even in her travels, she notes the possibility of becoming stale and stuck in the familiar. "I think at some point, perhaps, whatever vehicle you're in stops working for you—and then you need to try something else. The structure becomes too confining at some point."

Watson importantly adds the issue of context to make to know. The process is not only a matter of making work; the environment of that making has to be right. It needs to be challenging and fresh. "When you're exploring something new you are forced to problem-solve and navigate. Everything is new and there are many different paths, different contexts. You might take the wrong path—or the right one. It's a risk but involves thinking, searching and figuring it out." She references her life again and tells the story about how she and her husband, Mark Todd (a remarkable artist in his own right), left New York City after having lived there for five years in a deliberate attempt, once again, to shake things up. They moved upstate to the small hamlet of Ghent, "in the middle of nowhere" in Columbia County. They left what she calls the "habit loop" of New York City, and she asserts that this move to a new environment had a profound effect on her work. "That's when I started painting these landscapes that were ironic. It was this beautiful Americana landscape painted in the folk-art style that I was seeing at a lot of antique stores. We took this risk of moving and it changed our work, and many new things have sprung up from that. It is similar, for me, to a planned fire—to get rid of old growth and allow for new. It's like John Baldessari taking a chunk of his work and cremating it, so that he could start again." She then tells me stories about going on road trips with her family just to make art in new places, asking the same question over and over in each new destination.

I ask Watson what happens when she receives a call from, say, the *New York Times* with an illustration assignment, a commercial project. Is there a different process that ensues? She explains that often the client will need something specific and will give her a description. But in a spirit parallel to the novelist's "writing through" to discovery, Watson says, "I just get out a big old stack of 8.5 x 11 sheets of paper. I'll just start drawing. Just drawing. And I always know the first ideas are crap, and I will draw through them. The failures used to worry me when I was younger. But as I've gained my confidence, I know at the end of the day I will have something good. If I don't, by tomorrow morning I'll have something good. I'll just have to sleep on it. Most importantly, I just need to sit and keep drawing. And if it isn't working, that's all right. I just crumple it up. It's 8.5 x 11 paper." Her students ask her all the time how she gets to her ideas. "I tell them I just have to start. Draw through to find them. A lot of students are scared to start, unless they know exactly where they're going. I try to teach them that it rarely works that way." In the context of commercial work, Watson's make-to-know process is, curiously, as active as it is in any other part of her creative life. She engages material and situation. She "makes" from the unknown to the known.

Watson may not hold a vision of her work that she ultimately manifests; but she does acknowledge that sometimes she thinks about what

Esther Pearl Watson, *Red Barn*, created during her time in Ghent, NY. "This was the scene outside my studio window."

she wants her viewers to feel. "On occasion, I know what I want you to experience when you look at the work and what I want you to walk away feeling." But she distinguishes that feeling from the work itself. "I don't know exactly what the images are just yet, and I need to do some research and sketching to figure it out. I'll have to jump in to sketching and failures and all that to get to that moment where I think 'That's what I want you to feel when you see that piece.'"

I find the distinction intriguing—something relevant to Watson but completely foreign to an artist like Tom Knechtel, who, when I ask if he has ever had a vision of what he wants the viewer to *feel*, could not be clearer in his response: "Absolutely not." Watson, by contrast, discusses with me, in compelling detail, an example of a show she did in Texas in which she wanted the viewers to feel the residues of a particular history. "I wanted them to feel recognition of a memory for something that was faded, like maybe the smell of a car when the radiator is too hot or a real old house, walking into a really old wooden house. Things like that. Recognizing something that's gone—because I paint memories." By creating a distinction between a vision of what a work might be and the effect that a work might have, Watson makes more complex the question of vision in creative activity.

THE URGE TO MAKE/THE DESIRE TO KNOW

Whatever inspiration is, it's born from a continuous
"I don't know."
—WISŁAWA SZYMBORSKA[15]

The celebrated artist and illustrator Ann Field connects to her work from a place of intuition and feeling. She enters her projects by way of an internal awareness, a relationship, say, with a landscape, a photograph, or an image of beauty she might hold. It is an attentiveness that compels her to begin the making and, as it does, simultaneously creates for her a sense of restlessness.

"I feel like I'm getting a pull the whole time," Field tells me. "It's very powerful, and I feel upset and uncomfortable if I can't be doing it. It's very strong, and it seems like it's not my idea. It's almost as if it's somebody else's idea. It's magnetic."

"And when you feel that pull," I ask, "what happens?"

"I have to start making immediately, but that may not be with the planned thing. I'll just start trying to get something down. Begin to draw. Paint."

"Do you have a vision before the drawing?"

"Not precisely, but there is definitely an imprint. But not an exact one." And then, echoing Hamilton, she concludes, "It's a response thing."

"And then you give visual form to that response?"

"Yes, it's very clear to me that is exactly what it is. The feeling actually bothers me on some level. It's not complete happiness. But I have to do it. I'm compelled."

Field tells me that the "pull" she feels guides the making. But then, she says, at some point her "editorial mind" suddenly takes over, and she will either recalibrate her approach or "rescue" what she's done. And then she will draw some more. And edit. And so on. "You see what you need to do, whatever it's supposed to be, out of balance or in balance."

"When you finally encounter the form that you have drawn, is it a surprise?"

"It's not a surprise, no. It's not surprise. It's a recognition."

"That's exactly what Ann Hamilton said to me."

"Yeah, I *recognize* it. It's like it was there all the time but I had to find it, and then it comes out. It's not a chancy thing, but I've got to be all lined up to find it. I sometimes feel like these things are all images and designs that already exist. I just can't see them until I make them. That's really how I see, artistically."

Field grounds her comments in an example of being in a landscape and responding to her feelings of a particular world, experiencing the trees of that landscape and feeling some affinity. "They're very old living things and they have great character. But how to realize that experience, that feeling of affinity or connection? I could look at it as color. I could look at it as light. I could look at it as form only. But inside all that is really an individuality that I'm responding to, I think, in each tree. And beauty—that's probably the one word that is my core search in everything I do. I want my work to be beautiful, and compelled by beauty."

To get there, she creates a series of studies, draws through them, and works to find the one or two that might be right. "I may create up to eighty pieces before I get to something. And whether that actually takes the form of that tree, literally, is a push and pull. Parts of it will and parts of it won't."

Connectedness and affinity of internal sensation with the surrounding world, and the rehearsal of the many studies to find the recognized form, is only part of Field's story. There is also music. There is the body. There is encounter with material in what becomes almost a dance-like engagement. Like Watson, she reflects on the environment of the making, but with a twist: "Music is huge to me. Hugely important. I have to be listening to music, constantly. It just goes with my own sense of expressiveness of life, joy of life. Music is always with me when I'm working. It's like conducting. Like dance."

As she speaks, it all makes sense, what I see in her work and who she is: an artist of quality who responds deeply to intuitive impulses and to an understanding of all that stirs within as she encounters her world, her experience. And then she brings music into her process and feels a rhythm and finds that rhythm in the work itself. It is a quality that can only come through the making and is only of the moment. It is a rhythm *known* only in creation. As you look at the images of her work, you see ample evidence of the musicality and visual rhythm she achieves.

"Is each piece its own melody?" I ask her.

"A perfect piece *is* for me a melody. That's a great analogy. That's perfect."

Ann Field, *Blue Hair*. "My work, which is incredibly gestural, is almost like breath, like breathing."

105

"And what about the body, in that visually rhythmic, melodious world in which you create? Is it a form of dance in the making?"

"I use my body to work, standing up, gestural in my approach," she says. And then she brings many strands together by opening up in compelling detail about this aspect of her process: "I recognize my own life force in my body in movement. I don't consciously go about it this way, but I realize I need to bring all of my senses of being alive to the moment when I'm making something in order for it to succeed."

"When you imagine bringing yourself completely to it," I press her, "how and where does that manifest?"

"My work, which is incredibly gestural, is almost like breath, like breathing. You know it's a movement, like dance. In order for a line to have figure and flourish—what do they call it in France? Verve?—I have to bring physicality to it. And it is more pointed than just the rebel yell or the primordial thing. It's actually quite controlled as much as it is free."

I look at Field's work, and I am struck by her talent and skill. I am moved by its grace and stirred by its gentle buoyancy. However she gets there, to that point of recognition—through material engagement on the scaffolding of music, dance, intuition—the finding and discovery (the knowing) comes through only in the making and gives form to what is otherwise unknown. The passage from *A Midsummer Night's Dream* comes to mind once again. This is an artist, to be sure, who "gives to airy nothing/A local habitation and a name."

Chapter 4

DESIGNING THE "YET TO BE": PROBLEMS AND SOLUTIONS

Designing has been characterized as knowing through making or doing. It happens only as it is instantiated in the moment.
—POUL BITSCH OLSEN AND LORNA HEATON[1]

There exists a unique relationship between uncertainty and design activity. Because to design is to engage with an exploration of ideas towards the yet to be. Understanding this relationship is important if we are to develop our understanding of what it is to design.
—JAMES SELF[2]

What is make to know in the world of design? What happens when a project becomes fundamentally about solving a problem? What occurs when the imagination is geared toward conceiving a new future, creating change? How does designing products directly for a client, or for users, impact the creative process? How does one come to know through a making informed by empathy? These questions all emerge through the processes of design, and they open a distinctive point of view on entering uncertainty and the make-to-know experience.

To gain a real understanding of make to know in a design context, I've spoken with many different individuals: graphic designers, industrial designers, product designers, automobile designers, furniture designers, interaction designers, social impact designers, architects. Their stories are rich and their processes alive and complex. And what they articulate about the revelatory nature of their creative endeavors brings new insight into the making/knowing dynamic.

SOLVING PROBLEMS

The designers I have interviewed talk about their work primarily as solving problems.[3] This is fundamental to the way they think and move through their projects. One can equate the objective of problem-solving for these designers to the goal of winning for a professional athlete—it's axiomatic. We might imagine that the design process is about opening possibilities or inventing, formulating, devising, even discovering. All those terms are relevant, but always in service to problem-solving. That's what these designers do. To see the world through the lens of problems and solutions is to understand the context of how designers know through making.

The iPod is a commonly used, if now somewhat dated, example of how to understand design as a solution to a problem. From a designer's point of view, the making of that device solved "the problem" of people wanting to listen to music in public places. The iPod, easily portable from its first iteration and eventually simply a one-inch square that could be affixed to the user's clothing, made it easy to carry thousands of songs everywhere: to the park, to the gym, on the subway, even floating in a canoe on the lake. Our entire music collection would always be at hand. The project undoubtedly required advanced engineering and technological invention, but its ultimate purpose, its "why," its method of use, its availability for a mass market, its feel and look—all were design problems that required solutions. And, as time passed and technology advanced, designers found a further solution to the problem of multiple devices in the development of the smartphone, which soon had the capacity to incorporate every function of the original iPod.

Many of us involved in design education have for years attempted to explain the work of designers by saying things like: "Look around you. Someone has designed everything you see. The clothes you are wearing, the desk you are writing on, the plate you are using for food, the phone you are holding. Somebody thought about each one of those things, about how it might be used, how it could function optimally, how it might look and feel, the materials best to use, the resources required to manufacture it, the implications for sustainability, and so on." Each one of those elements presented a problem to solve. And each problem was part of a larger one that the designer was attempting to address—the problem of safeguarding bodies (clothing), or the problem of needing a surface for work (desk), or the problem of expedient and rapid communication (smartphone), and so forth.

Consider the reflections of designer Anne Burdick on how she might go about designing a Coca-Cola bottle. She speaks in terms of problems and the choreography of solutions. "Let's say I'm creating a prototype out of clay or through 3D printing. As I'm working on it, I'm thinking about how it fits in the box for shipping or how it feels in the hand. The designer of a mass-produced product, especially something as pervasive as a Coke bottle, considers multiple problems with multiple ramifications. And I know if I pull it a little more this way, I make it a little fatter. And by doing that, I have just affected how many bottles can fit in a shipping container. And if I push it more another way, it's too far from the brand identity. Or if I change it a little bit more in this direction, it will be more ecologically friendly." The ripple effect of each choice in the design process is extensive and complicated. The designer is not simply the person in the system who was hired to create a shape or to make something "look good"—the latter being the most common misconception about the essential work of design. The designer is someone whose process can influence myriad elements that have serious, complex consequences for significant issues like global supply chains, brand identity, waste management, and even shareholder interest.

Design is, by definition, knowing through making. It is, as designers repeatedly tell me, about multiple failures that form a pathway to success. It is exploratory in its essence, crafted to lead to unexpected discoveries along the way, or to motivate both client and designer to revisit fundamental assumptions.

THE CORE PROBLEM

Graphic designer Sean Adams tells an illuminating story about problem-solving in his design of the logo he created for the VH1 network. "The first thing I did was look at the network itself and quickly realized it was lacking. They were doing terrible specials, bad comedy reviews, and reruns of old shows that were cheap. They had lost their focus on music. I sat down with a group of executives and tried to get at what they *thought* they were about. At first the answer was 'We are the sister network to MTV.'" That vague response, at best defining identity through comparison to something external, together with the inferior and unfocused programming Adams witnessed, gave him a clear insight into a deeper problem that he needed to solve. The issue was not simply one of creating a logo. The pressing matter had to do with the fundamental question of identity.

And it was Adams, the designer, who pointed out the problem. "The executives insisted they just needed a logo, as if that would fix everything. I knew I could give them a nice logo, but it would do nothing. Ratings would continue to drop. And I might be blamed for that. I wouldn't have solved a problem at all."

Adams framed for VH1 the single question he wanted them to address: "What can you as VH1 own that defines who you are?" From there a conversation ensued among them and, as Adams tells it, they "eventually realized that they could own the history of American popular music. MTV could not do that. MTV was about newness and youth. VH1 could own the classics. And, in the end, that discovery informed the identity of the entire graphic system. The logo ended up having the VH1 mark," Adams recounts, "but underneath it, it said, 'Music First.' It was a marker, a reminder that they were fundamentally about music, in a focused way, which did not include superfluous programming external to the core mission."

Sean Adams, VH1 logo
design, 1998.

The implications here about design are enormously important. The process of designing an identity system was, in this case, ultimately a process of identifying and solving a problem of self-knowledge and organizational focus. The designer helped shape this work, something essential to the company's ultimate success. VH1 went on to create projects like "Behind the Music" or "Concert of the Century" and similar programming pertinent to the history of American popular music. Adams sums up the essential focus of his work with refreshing clarity: "What is the problem we are trying to solve? What are we really getting at? Those are the questions that need to be addressed—as opposed to superficially slapping an image onto an organization."

RESEARCH AS MAKING

Understanding what problem to solve emerges, at least partly, through a process of design research. But the designers interviewed for this book do not see a simple cause-and-effect relationship between research and problem identification, at least not at its core. Designers, moreover, rarely consider research as a prelude to an engaged making that comes at a later time in the studio. Research—and knowing the problem to solve—is part of the making. It is dynamic and creative. It is a multidimensional activity that includes generative questions about such things as cultural context, market need, technological possibility, user experience, economic circumstance, budgetary constraint, regulatory environment, material possibility and the like. The research process in design is nuanced and non-linear. It leads to ideation that often stimulates further research, changes previous assumptions, opens new conversations and collaborations (with engineers, business partners, social innovators, or marketers). Those collaborations in turn layer on new ideas. It twists and turns in a kaleidoscope of possibility. Research is part of a complex composition.

Designer Tisha Johnson—who at the time of our conversation was vice president for interior design at Volvo, although she has since moved on—tells me about a certain category of projects in her industry that are quite deliberately open and improvisational. These endeavors intentionally leverage making not just to know the product itself, but also to discover new creative research paths toward developing it. They illustrate beautifully the ways in which research functions as part of making in design, opening discovery about both process and product. Projects like this take on a "skunkworks" feel; they are deliberately created to use research as an open and creative part of the work. It is fascinating to think about such an improvised journey when it comes, of all things, to designing a car.

"We don't really have a clear brief," Johnson explains. "We generate the brief through research, through discovering what we must design for, or answer to. We don't come to the table with any assumptions. It will start very broad. It can be, for example, about a given generation or an emerging technology. And we pursue it. We read and research and talk. It might be that we notice the convergence of several things that focus our thinking. It really is about discovering the problem that we need to solve."

It is striking that here we have an industry, immense and highly structured, that is keenly interested in process and experimentation and in a kind of making not just to know a product but to define a problem. It might seem counterintuitive, but research, when thought about as making, is not so much a preparatory intellectual exercise as it is, for designers, a deeply creative one woven into the entire process.

THE TESLA MODEL S

The connection that Johnson describes between research and making in automobile design is beautifully illustrated in a story told to me by Tesla's chief designer, Franz von Holzhausen. It is a story of how he faces uncertainty, how he sketches his way to his fundamental guiding questions, and how he ultimately finds his inspiration. But in those very processes, his is also a story of the research/making process in the spirit of the Volvo projects described by Johnson.

"When I joined Tesla in 2008," von Holzhausen recalls, "it was the end of the summer. It was August. And immediately I stepped into the exploration of the Model S and what it was going to be. In truth, it was wide open, and I equate the moment to the blank sheet of paper that a writer faces at the outset of a novel. It's a pretty daunting and challenging task. But I took that on as an opportunity to think about basic principles of the Model S, finding the guiding light. I always look first for the soul of the projects I work on."

"So how did you go about it?"

"Many of the electric cars in 2008 were like spaceships. Some of them had three wheels, kind of odd, kind of non-automotive-looking products. Potentially great for early adopters, but that's probably it." Von Holzhausen believed he had a clean slate and needed to find an entry point. He thought about the fundamental mission of Tesla the company and its focus on efficiency and electric propulsion. And, like many of the artists and designers I've spoken to, von Holzhausen wrestled with fundamental questions that served as his way in. "How do I describe visually what that mission means in physical terms? What is efficiency about? It could be efficiency in mode, in traffic, in production. How quickly can we move? How cleanly can we move? And how do I translate that into a visual language?"

With those questions propelling him forward, he began his research—on his bicycle! "The Tour de France had just happened. I'm a cyclist, and I was riding a lot. This idea came into my head, during a ride, that these professional cyclists, they're all about efficiency. They are finely tuned machines. Their physique is sculpted to match the performance that's required. They are sprinters. They have endurance. They go long distance. They go against the odds of physical capacity of normal humans. The end result is this kind of motion of a beautiful physique. That became the soul, the essence for the design language of the Model S. I just kept trying to capture lean muscle mass, the highly tuned form, and turn it back into a sculpture that became the vehicle. Look at the lines of the fenders, the really lean body mass. It translates into efficiency." Efficiency of the body—finding this was an integral part of von Holzhausen's research. It was creative and engaged.

Many of the designers I speak to offer a corrective to how we might think about research in any project, in any field. What design clarifies is that making is a broad and multifaceted activity. "Research as prelude" is equivalent to limiting the creative enterprise to the formulaic "vision to execution" myth that I have tried to debunk throughout this book. In design, research and the generation of ideas are inseparable, non-linear, mutually nourishing—part of the making.

One significant aspect of design research cited by several of my interviewees is the dialogue designers enter into with each other, as well as with engineers, with marketplaces, with history, with culture. Dialogue was certainly part of the creative journey for von Holzhausen while he was designing the Model S. He tells me about entering a dialogue with the electric cars that already existed at that time. He wanted the Model S to "talk to" those vehicles and to build on their aesthetic. "I felt efficiency was important to communicate visually simply because anybody looking at the electric car at that time (and even now) would say, 'Of course these other cars can't go the distance. They are blocky, heavy-looking vehicles.' By contrast, I wanted to create this sense of lightness on wheels, of powerful proportion, of a beautiful physique. There's not an ounce of fat on that vehicle. It's a finely tuned, refined, sculpted feel of hips and shoulders and a lean waist. It gives a feeling of motion even while standing still."

He also used the term "dialogue" to describe his engagement with nature, with thoroughbred horses, cheetahs in motion, or hawks in flight. "Their physiques change in motion to a kind of perfection. And I tried to achieve that same essence in the overall design. And that's what you see on the road today. I think it's the most aerodynamic design on the market. The car is a sprinter. It translates efficiency into sculpture."

Tesla Model S, 2009.

CURIOSITY

My interview with the venerable and internationally recognized architect Frank Gehry begins with a lament on his part that people in his profession have become disconnected from their roots in artistic tradition. With more than a hint of sadness, he says: "Architects have forgotten their heritage, that they were artists, and the world has diminished as a result."

Gehry believes passionately in the importance of artists wrestling with complex and profound questions, something he considers fundamental to his own career and to the research he conducts. For him, the disconnect between architects and their artistic heritage leads to the production of architectural work that lacks the power and beauty great questions can yield. It's the particular curiosity of the artist that Gehry wants to possess as an architect, and he wants others in his profession to aim for this too. Asking great questions born of deep curiosity is the entry point, for him, into the uncertainty of the creative space. Such questions shape his research and are an essential part of his making— the making that is the path to knowing.

"Curiosity is what I think starts it all. Talmudic scholarship is the model I use. That form of learning is all about questions that lead to questions. And those Talmudic scholars never gave up. I'm not religious, but I was always struck that everything starts with a question. What's right for this? What should I do? What kind of space is this? Where is it? How does it fit in the surrounding space? How should it relate to people?" Gehry goes on to explain that his experience and education give shape to those questions, catalyzing his movement through them.

I recognize in Gehry's reflections the same principle I cited earlier— experience, education, values, priorities, ethics, even talent, all create the scaffolding on which the individual stands to enter what remains unknown until the making. The artist's experience and background do not resolve ambiguity or answer questions; they give the creative individual, the designer/architect in this case, a substantive way to reach for discovery, to *address* the questions. Great questions open up possibilities. Experience furthers the reach.

The designer Frido Beisert likewise talks about curiosity as a fundamental trait of his work in design. Beisert is a consummate design instructor who operates a boutique concept design consultancy in Los Angeles. His experience is wide-ranging and includes developing futuristic video games, being an underground DJ, and writing a book on learning design using 3D software.

"I always start with the question," Beisert tells me. "And it is usually a 'what if' question. That is my brief. That is what motivates me. The question is what gives energy to move in a certain direction. 'What if I do this?'" Designers have constant radar for new questions, new possibilities, new problems to solve. Beisert reveals this constant in his life: "I'm seeing things here in your room," he says to me during the interview, "just sitting here, that are giving me ideas, just because my curiosity drives me there. And every night at dinner my wife and I have conversations that yield a list of ten to twelve different things that we want to contemplate, work on, maybe design for our business or explore further for other projects."

Beisert fills his life with questions born of curiosity, questions that he constructs as potential problems to solve. And they are questions, as Sean Adams would say, that are penetrating and specific enough to get at substantive issues—they will not simply produce a "canned response."

RESEARCH AS DIALOGUE

One of the freshest insights to emerge from my interviews with designers was about dialogue. Designers, as noted earlier, often find themselves engaged in multiple dialogues while they make to know. It is common for them to talk about taking an empathic approach to their work, and about the user experience being fundamental to any design they create.

User experience (UX) design requires of the designer a sophisticated research methodology governed by human-centered awareness of the product's ultimate users, their needs, and the problems they need to solve. That observation is not particularly new. But what I discovered during my exploration of make to know is that any design research process, and the UX research process in particular, comprises multiple dialogues in which designers engage. They weave those dialogues together to form the basic fabric of investigation.

Specifically, designers are in dialogue with engineers, with clients, with business developers, with marketers; but they are also often in "dialogue" with more conceptual things like current technology, trends in colors and materials, the work or products of other designers; or with culture, history, a marketplace, and so on. Designers frequently talk about their process in these dialogic terms.

Tisha Johnson, for example, reflects on how much she draws strength from a basic lesson about dialogic discovery from the early days of her creative education, a lesson that echoes the significant process of material engagement discussed in Chapter 3. She tells me about the first figure-drawing class she ever took, well before she studied design. The instructor of that class taught her something that has stayed with her throughout her career, something that is perfectly aligned with the make-to-know experience: "The instructor described within the first few days the dialogue that one has with the material. She stressed how the person creating the drawing may very well not have a clear picture in his or her head about what it is going to be. But then something happens; the artist strikes the object. In this case, it is charcoal moving against the grit of paper. And in that moment, you get something back that is unexpected. It speaks to you. And she described it as a conversation. She would say, 'Oh, you gave me that. I'll give you this.'" Johnson goes on to elucidate how important that lesson was to her, and how deeply it still informs her work as a designer today. "It helps me feel comfortable in the process of discovery, in the making of the thing. It makes me comfortable even when I'm terribly uncomfortable not having the answer. There's a whole lot of unknown that ends up impacting the process and that causes me to make many turns along the way."

My conversation with Frank Gehry expands and deepens this insight into some of the conceptual exchanges in which the designer participates. He talks to me about the ways in which a design might interact with the surrounding architecture of a given project, or with the history of a given city. His language is quite deliberate: "to be in dialogue" with the right buildings or with the history of a place.

He offers an example from a current project he is working on in his home city of Toronto. He has had a disagreement with the city regarding a small warehouse building and a debate about its historical significance. For Gehry, the focus on that building took attention away from the "dialogue I needed for the design." Like a writer, this architect creates a kind of conversation among his "characters": other buildings, architectural histories, landscapes, surrounding structures. "I showed the values of Union Station, the Royal York Hotel, and the Parliament Houses. Those were the buildings in Toronto that I grew up with. That's my image of Canada, of Toronto." In the end, he focused on a design that, in his words, "*would talk to* old Toronto."

Frank Gehry, Toronto King Street building project. Design process began in 2018. Rendering by Sora. Gehry Partners, LLP.

Frank Gehry, 8 Spruce Street (formerly known as Beekman Tower) with the Manhattan skyline, 2011. Gehry Partners, LLP.

This idea of his buildings "talking to" all that surrounds them is intriguing. I think a comparison with the novelist or playwright is apt. The exchange and interaction among characters and even, as we have seen, between characters and writers, is all part of the creative cosmology. It is a stimulus for discovery. Gehry goes on to give examples of some of his projects from New York, Bilbao, and Abu Dhabi. As he speaks, there is at least a hint of theatrical language. "The building I did at Beekman in New York. You need to look at it in relation to the Woolworth Building and the Brooklyn Bridge. It becomes an *ensemble*. And when I went to Bilbao, I told them I wanted to study their history, and their culture, which I did. I was able to communicate with the people, work with them. I respected their environment."

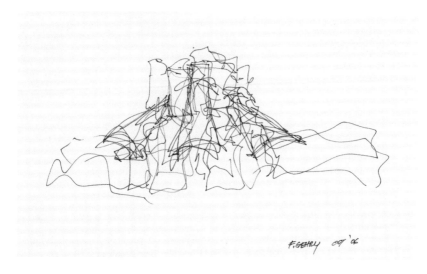

F.GEHRY 09 '06

Frank Gehry, Guggenheim Abu Dhabi museum sketch and model.
Design process began in 2006. Gehry Partners, LLP.

The design for the much-delayed Guggenheim Abu Dhabi was a
product of ten to fifteen different models that Gehry experimented with,
and that took shape in the concept phase of his work—but always in
conversation with his clients on the one hand and the city, the culture,
the history on the other. "I made all these studies—what if, what if, what
if, what if—just searching for their response." When Abu Dhabi finally
chose one of the models, they did so because "they believed I had fundamentally understood their culture." The design emerged through an
extensive and multifaceted dialogue.

MULTIPLE DIALOGUES

The presence of a client is a specific aspect of the design process that many interviewees identify as distinguishing the designer's work from that of the fine artist. Industrial designer Andy Ogden, for example, focuses when we talk on his dialogue with the client, how fundamental it is to his work, and how deeply it connects to the problem-solving mentality he carries. "I started in the field of art, making things that I thought were interesting expressions, or that I simply wanted to make. Those projects didn't solve a problem and were not prescribed by somebody else's goals or needs. It turns out that I am someone who resonates with learning about something that is a problem to solve; that's the thing that I'm interested in. It's a puzzle; it's a game; there's something fun about that."

As he proceeds to discuss his process, it becomes wholly evident that solving the puzzle must include a dialogue with the client, customer, or tacit collaborator. "I build a conceptual framework that has some goals, and I always use a value framework that focuses on the customer in the situation, the client, or the company. I teach a practice that calls on the designer to manage the various values of the stakeholders. It's imperative to engage that way if the designer is going to be successful. You need to build within someone else's framework. And there's something expressive within that, and it's part of my drive." Building in another's framework: an essential element of make to know in design.

Intriguingly, however, make to know is for Ogden not just something that happens on one side of the dialogue. The client does it as well, and is a full participant. "I think the make-to-know process is a truth, not something that some are practicing, some are not. And whether the client knows it or not, they are going through the same process. Part of the reason they are hiring a designer is because they too need to make to know."

This insight is noteworthy, and ultimately complicates our understanding of the design-making process. The importance of considering another—developing the "empathy muscle," as some designers like to say—is indisputable. It's the familiar way designers get to an important level of their process and sense of the user. In the words of interaction designer Maggie Hendrie: "Understanding for me, personally, includes empathy. I understand people when I'm watching them use technology. I understand their little joys and frustrations and their grimaces. Understanding for me includes emotional engagement." With this kind of understanding, the argument goes, good design stands a chance.

But, like Ogden, Hendrie extends our thinking about the design process into a much fuller kind of dialogue with the client. It's not simply an "observe and learn" engagement that builds empathy. It's actually a deep and important conversation that goes into much more complex territory. In her words: "I'm interested in participatory design and the co-creation of meaning." When Hendrie is working with a client, she does it in a way "that makes the other person understand that not only is there going to be an outcome, they are going to participate in it."

In this way, make to know in design is fundamentally collaborative. Writers and visual artists enter into uncertainty, into a space of negative capability, that functions like a creative playground of discovery—but they are often operating on their own, through a process of making that stimulates individual imagination. Designers, on the other hand, enter into a dialogue with the client or user (and certainly many others), and this dialogue is an essential part of the fabric of their discovery and creation.

Designer Nik Hafermaas tells a fascinating tale about his work on a project called *Dazzle,* a piece he created for the 1,600-foot building façade of the Rental Car Center at San Diego International Airport. It is a story that demonstrates with great clarity the significance of the exchange and deep dialogue that a designer can go through with a variety of "interlocutors," and how fundamentally that can inform the evolution of a project.

In the early days of the project, Hafermaas suspected that he had been hired to "decorate" something, to make "the façade look pretty," as he explains it. "The money allocated by the client was for a landmark art piece that was somehow going to enhance the situation, visually. But no one thought or even hinted at the possibility of anything beyond that, of touching the façade physically or doing something that required some action. I could have placed an oversized flower bouquet next to it or made things that would flap in the wind—or something equally uninspired."

Hafermaas didn't want anything to do with some clichéd product that would yield "the expected result." He also didn't have a "vision," and he knew he needed a *making* process to discover what he could produce that was different and exciting. He saw his work as engaging with the client in a fuller way, in a manner that challenged them. "How can I change? How can I change the game?" He loved that challenge, and he knew that it had to come from a very specific creative process with his client. "I'm not going to bother with something unless I see the opportunity to really have an impact, make a change."

Hafermaas brought to this project, in his words, a "subversive" agenda. But in his discussion with me, he later recharacterizes his approach as something closer to "subversive playfulness." The latter word is an important modification because, beyond the creative meanings of "playfulness," the idea also connotes to him the open dialogue of a play. "It's a subversive approach that is also playful. I play in open-ended experimentation. It's also a play designed to see where it leads you—the ability to role-play with others, in dialogue. And then it's a play because it's performance. Can I engage a client or stakeholder beyond where they are normally willing to go?"

Hafermaas sought to create a design for the façade that would be more exciting in texture and dimension than the original architecture. He wanted to work against the conventional. In his "performance" with the client, he referenced the idea of Dazzle camouflage—a type of ship camouflage used in the First and Second World Wars, originally invented by English artist Norman Wilkinson while he was serving in the Royal Navy Volunteer Reserve. Dazzle camouflage consists of patterns of geometric shapes painted onto ships in a variety of intersecting forms. The idea, historically, was not so much about camouflage in the familiar sense of concealment; it had more to do with making a ship's target range, speed, or direction difficult to read or to estimate. In Wilkinson's words, the objective was for a ship to

Dazzle battleship: FFS *Gloire*, 1944.

be painted "not for low visibility, but in such a way as to break up her form and thus confuse [an enemy] submarine officer as to the course on which she was heading."[4]

In a similar spirit, Hafermaas brought the concept of Dazzle camouflage into the San Diego Airport project not to hide the façade, but to give it form and dimension that would, in his words, "scramble its appearance" and solve the problem of its commonplace design. Ultimately, he wanted to defamiliarize the architecture and create an interactive experience with the building. "And to my great surprise," he tells me, "they said they loved the concept. Even the architect was intrigued. I told him, 'You designed the building and gave it a grid. I'm going to go against that grid, challenge our perception.' And I left that presentation with the green light to follow the Dazzle camouflage idea."

"How did the idea come to you in the first place?" I ask.

"I was flipping through the pages of my favorite German car magazine, *Intersection Magazine*. I found by sheer accident a small article on Dazzle camouflage. I became curious about using this technique not on a moving object—a ship—but on a stationary façade. I wasn't interested in hiding the façade, but in scrambling our perception of it."

"An accident?"

"In one sense, yes. But in another sense, I was actively engaged in making this thing. I was receptive to all ideas."

Here surfaces another example of that "happy accident" that so many artists and designers reference in their work. As I suggested earlier, however, "accident" might be a misnomer. The seemingly random, as Amy Tan points out, emerges in a cosmology of creativity—as if there is a kind of law that brings it into being. To use Hamilton's language, it requires responsiveness on the part of the artist, readiness.

The rest of the story that took this project to its conclusion is one of experimentation and prototyping to find the right material to realize the concept. Hafermaas dismissed the idea of simply painting the façade to accomplish the goal. "That is a cheap way of achieving the camouflage," he told me (although it should be remembered that painting was the way Wilkinson originally created Dazzle camouflage). He wanted it to be animated, brought to life. And so he first experimented with using a black film material that reflects interesting shapes when light shines on it. "The idea was that cars driving by would animate it by virtue of their headlights. We tried it, through a full-scale prototype, but it just didn't work." And then serendipity—another "happy accident"—took over again.

"I got a phone call from the people at E Ink Corporation, who create the screens of the Kindle reader, the e-paper display," Hafermaas explained. "They had seen previous work of mine. They said, we like your work and we have this material. You know it from Kindle readers. And now we can print this out a mile long. We don't know what to do with it. We need your help. And then, at that very second, on the phone, I said, 'Yeah, I think I know what we're going to do.' I went back to the airport and asked, 'How about we animate the whole thing?' I explained to them how this electronic paper would work. It's a passive display. It actually has little molecules that can turn between black and white. Can you imagine doing this for an exterior of a façade?"

Hafermaas joined forces with fellow artists Dan Goods and David Delgado from NASA's Jet Propulsion Laboratory and they entered into a long research and development phase to test the material, determining

Dazzle project at San Diego International Airport's
Rental Car Center, 2017.

what would be needed to expose it to the elements for an extended
time. Through prototyping they were able to develop an actual working
product. In the end, a unique design emerged comprising hundreds
of tiles (produced by E Ink Corporation) that combined photovoltaic
material with a special weatherized e-paper, strategically placed onto
the building. It was far too expensive to wallpaper the entire façade
with these tiles, and therefore the problem became one of how to create
maximum visual impact with the minimum quantity of material. As
seen from the images included here, the result is quite powerful. "There
is no other 1,600-foot-long façade made out of this technology on the
planet," Hafermaas tells me, "and it is completely solar powered. Has
no cable running. Has zero light pollution. Not like Times Square. Just
blasts of light through green technology."

It's notable just how many levels of dialogue were involved in the make-to-know process of this project. The dialogue between client and designer, and between designer and original architect, is obvious, as is the interchange among the artists and engineers involved. But it goes so much further. Hafermaas points out that his work was in dialogue with other, similar architectural façades (and the differentiation involved), and with multiple materials in new combinations and contexts. Curiously, the work also gave rise to a dialogue with the history of San Diego itself. According to the research Hafermaas conducted, Dazzle camouflage was first tested for effectiveness in the waters of San Diego. He was thus interested in the exchange with that history and, given the context of the airport, with the dialogue "where air meets water." This was a conversation of things fixed and in motion, of the hidden and the seen, of light and dark, of absorption and reflection. It was also, Hafermaas insists at the end of our conversation, "a dialogue with art history, with Norman Wilkinson himself, and the inspiration of cubism on his concept of Dazzle camouflage."

One more example of how designers work in dialogue is evident in the story of the development of an award-winning chair designed by David Mocarski for the company Gunlocke. He received a brief from the client that essentially called for "a simple bentwood chair with a unique personality." Mocarski tells me about his initial frustration with the vagueness of this brief, and about how he then immediately began the interesting process of complicating it as a way get to his design. His story gives evidence not only of how the creative process unfolds, even with the slightest direction, but also of the designer's role in bringing the client to greater understanding and knowing. As pointed out by Andy Ogden earlier in this chapter, there's a make-to-know journey for the client as well.

Mocarski began his process by entering into a dialogue with history. "I first started looking at the history of woodworking and craft of a lot of the European makers who came over to the United States and settled in Michigan and North Carolina. That's really where American furniture started. I was interested in their unique making process, a simplified process." This initial exploration then turned into a dialogue (in a manner that recalls Hafermaas discovering Dazzle camouflage by "accident") with another recognized cultural icon from the 1920s, the "Little Black Dress" of Coco Chanel. "I found myself thinking about the simplicity of the silhouette of the dress. I love the proportions. It's letting the figure essentially express itself through the dress, and the dress express itself through the figure."

This dialogue between crafted furniture and a versatile and affordable fashion design engaged Mocarski as he sketched ideas. His process unfolded simultaneously with a conversation among many tangible and intangible interlocutors. "Everything is happening at the same time. There's never a single linear thread. Everything has multiple layers. Any

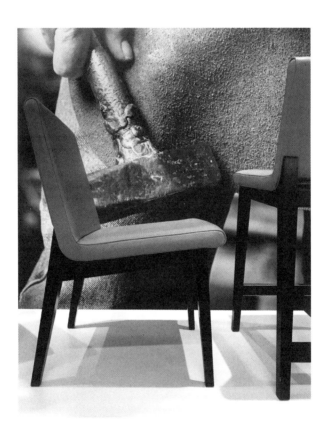

David Mocarski, Tia guest chair
produced by Gunlocke, 2017.

Chanel "Little Black Dress" illustration that appeared
in *Vogue* in 1926. © Conde Nast.

one question always has multiple answers and multiple possibilities. I'm constantly moving between thinking about context, or a particular brand, or what somebody else has done—and all those things are rotating through my mind as I'm drawing. And I also write. I write all my drawings. I'll write a single word sometimes. I write phrases. It's the way I play with the ideas. *It's me talking to the idea. It's the idea talking back to me.* That's when the magic happens. That's why at that point there's a creative process. That's problem-solving, and then there's a sort of innovation I can enter which, for me, is really that borderline place between magic and alchemy."

Make to know in design is discourse, movement, research, discussion, negotiation. It is sketching and model-building and writing and playing. It is conversing with culture and history. It is dialogue. It is collaboration with a team of fellow designers, engineers, business partners. It's about a conversation with the client, the company, the user. But, as Frido Beisert indicates, it's also a dialogue that exists among various media that he employs in his process. In Beisert's words: "The key thing for me is the transfer of medium. If I look at the evolution of an idea to a finished thing, I witness that it has undergone multiple stages of evolving. It's similar to a butterfly going through metamorphosis. Every time I transfer medium, I'm excited because it changes things. It alters the conversation. Sometimes the idea will be eliminated. Sometimes it gets better." Or, as designer Anne Burdick believes, making in design is a dialogue with objects, with the text of a book she is designing, as well as other people: "I have two kinds of collaborators. One is actual people. The other is text."

Until I began working on this book I never fully understood how much designers, like writers, create a world of conversation during their creative process—how parts of the process "talk" to one another. And it is only through multiple threads of dialogue that many designers find their way to the solution of a problem. There's a parallel to be made with Socratic dialogue (also a problem-solving strategy), but in the form of physical making. Far from knowing the solution from the beginning or possessing a vision to manifest, designers enter into a process of making that is dynamic and, at times, dialectical.

But the conversations are also, to me, theatrical. Designers might have Socrates in them through evidence of how they work, but they are also, more directly, like playwrights. They manage multiple dialogues, scenes, and characters that yield worlds and multilayered concepts. How little I understood, before I asked the make-to-know question, of this affinity between my designer colleagues' creative processes and the theatrical world in which I am trained and through which I have learned so much about human experience. Hamlet's declaration can now hold a new association, with all puns implied: "The play's the thing." It is indeed.

SKETCHING, MODELING, PROTOTYPING
My hand explains to myself what goes on in my mind.
—SAUL STEINBERG[5]

First there is the making, then there is the matching.
—E.H. GOMBRICH[6]

Designers make through various media, physical and digital, to find their way. They sketch ideas. They build models. They prototype and test. One architect might use blocks to explore the relationship of form in three-dimensional space, while another might play with one of several software programs for 3D modeling. Designers will almost always build prototypes of their designs as a central means of iterating and making. They build to discover. They think through physical shapes. They learn through material. They know through making.

When the architect Michael Maltzan walks me through his make-to-know process, he makes it clear that he engages in a number of different revelatory dialogues along the way. Like Gehry, with whom he worked early in his career, Maltzan is keenly aware of context and how his emerging design might find meaning in "the characteristics of a place," how it might "talk to" that place. It all begins for Maltzan with a notion or idea that he needs to put down physically. "And by physically, I mean it can even be a sketch on paper or iPad." As he speaks, I begin to understand that this process of "physicalizing" is a way for him to begin a conversation not unlike the ones we have when we're trying to get to know another person. In fact, he uses the word "vulnerable" to describe what happens in the first stages of expressing even a "notional idea." "It is first a willingness to be vulnerable in a more visible or public way. That beginning process of design, I think, is one which I have to struggle with—communicating something I am not a hundred percent certain about, but that might lead ultimately to something more."

"Many artists talk about this early phase as building a frame for deeper work," I say. "Is that how you see it?"

"For me, it's a physical declaration. I don't know how else to describe it. It's a declaration that reveals something incomplete residing in me, which I find very difficult to work when it's too much inside." And then he brings in the idea of a dialogue: "As soon as it is out, I can begin to work on it, bring my capabilities, tools, experiences. It's really a dialogue, in that it starts to be another character. It talks back to you."

If the sketch leads to something workable, if the vulnerable idea begins to take on substance through honest dialogic engagement, Maltzan will then attempt to create another level of conversation in three-dimensional form. "I try to move it from something two-dimensional to three-dimensional. That can be as simple as a small model of the idea. Maybe it's a little bit more fleshed out. It doesn't have to be large. But for me, it really has to be physical. The thing I'm interested in—and this may sound a little funny from an architect—is less the form and more the space that the form makes." Making this point, Maltzan communicates to me the significance of another intensified dialogue that is integral to his making process. "Either between the forms, or in the existing context around it—the space within or under or over the building—to me, that's where the meaning or the storyline is. It's hard and often less tangible, and often less visible to people. But that is what I'm after."

His engagement with the physical form, his dialogue with it, and the conversation that form has with its surroundings, is quite deliberately expressed as a making that leads to a knowing. "I have a sense of what I'm after, but I don't necessarily know what the right form is going to be to carry that ambition. And I often find that those first physical forms do not carry that ambition in the way that I wanted them to. I don't think I have an idea of the correct appearance, the correct aesthetic, but I do think I have a sense of what I'm trying to get at with the building."

"Is the modeling a way of knowing the idea? Or even what it shouldn't be? Does that language make any sense?"

"I do think it allows you to know it, and very often it allows you to know what it is not. It gives me a sense of the next step. Sometimes you scrap it entirely, but often it is more recalibrating it as a next step."

As our interview continues, I become aware that for Maltzan the iterative making process, the investigative dialogue, is fundamental. "It's in that process that you get not only to the building but to the continuity of ideas and beliefs and ambitions. That's the ongoing storyline. It's very hard for me to think of the design as being fixed. I don't really enjoy going out to the site and seeing things built, because during that part of the process, for many logistical and rational economic reasons, I can't make changes. I can tweak things, but I can't make changes. And yet when I'm there, it's impossible for me not to think of it still as a part of the process unfolding. I inevitably want to change things and move things around. But that has to stop." The evolution of the work ends for Maltzan sometime during the construction document process, "when I realize I really can't make changes anymore."

One final clarifying point about Maltzan's practice surfaces toward the end of our conversation. He insists that the distinct phases of his process, although manifesting in different forms of expression, are interlocking and do not necessarily proceed in sequence. He offers the example of the relationship between his sketches and the three-dimensional models upon which he relies so heavily. "I don't draw sketches and then make models from those sketches. I actually work on the model simultaneously, as if I'm sculpting with the models." In doing this, Maltzan creates a dialogue between the two-dimensional and the three-dimensional; his making process is a conversation between these different elements. The process focuses his work and ultimately brings it to a place of precision.

Frank Gehry is well known for his construction of three-dimensional models to further his designs. "I want to see it visually. I want to see the site. I want to see the relationships. Photographs don't do it for me; they help, but they don't complete the picture."

I ask him about the famous stories concerning his improvising with materials, crumpling up pieces of paper and throwing them on the floor as a way to find inspiration for the design of a building. "That happened," he tells me with a wry smile, "because of that TV thing that I'm on. They concocted that idea."

"*The Simpsons*?"

"Yeah, in the episode I get a letter asking me to design a concert hall for their town. I read it, crumple the paper and throw it on the ground. I then look at it, pick it up and say, 'Frank Gehry, you're a genius.'" The producers recorded Gehry's voice for the episode. But that last self-aggrandizing line, he goes on to tell me, was tough for him to say and it made for a lot of grief on the part of the director. "I couldn't say it with the conviction they wanted, because of course I'm Jewish and I don't believe it. But once that show aired, everybody thinks I crumple paper, and that's how I design. People used to stop me on the street. They would crumple a little paper and ask me to sign it."

Frank Gehry on *The Simpsons* (Season 16, Episode 14),
"The Seven-Beer Snitch," 2005. 'THE SIMPSONS' © 2005
Twentieth Century Fox Television. All rights reserved.

In reality, Gehry does experiment and improvise through sketching and modeling. These are crucial steps in the making and in the design. They bring him closer to a sense of what the building might be. But while we are discussing his sketches in particular, he says something quite striking—something that I initially think might just be a throwaway line. It's only as I reflect on the remark that I realize its significance. "I do sketch a lot," he says, "but I think the sketches would not be clear to anybody in terms of what I mean. If you looked at them, you wouldn't understand them."

This personal and almost idiosyncratic idea of the sketch interests me. "I can just start thinking about things through sketching," says Andy Ogden, "and I can create a symbology that I understand and use to wrestle with the problems." But, like Gehry, Ogden specifies: "I'm not making a drawing for someone else to see. I'm making symbols for me to think through something." Michael Maltzan mentions the "vulnerability" of his early sketches, while Frido Beisert, intriguingly, asserts that he can read the personal in the sketches of any designer: "I'm a firm believer that I can look at someone's sketchbook and tell who they are."

On one level, the idiosyncratic nature of sketches clearly reflects the raw early work that some designers use to enter a space of creative uncertainty. It's simply the initial stages, not ready for prime time. The reflections of these designers remind me of the novelists I discussed in an earlier chapter. Their drawings are equivalent to the pages of writing that, for example, Tom Stern uses to find out something about a character that interests him. It is a stage of the process in which the conceptual can evolve through the physical or material, and it is not meant for anyone but the creator, the maker. It is the sculptor Alexander Calder thinking in wire.

But it is personal on another level as well, one that is significant to the make-to-know experience. What artists and designers come to know in the making is not only what the work itself needs to be, but often something about themselves and how they think or feel about a given idea, question, or struggle. Joan Didion exemplifies this self-learning most powerfully when grieving the sudden loss of her husband, John Gregory Dunne, and, a year and a half later, her daughter, Quintana

Roo Dunne. As her longtime book editor, Shelley Wanger, says in a 2017 documentary about Didion, "Joan needs to write to know how she thinks."[7] In Didion's own words, "Had I been blessed with even limited access to my own mind there would have been no reason to write."[8] She created *The Year of Magical Thinking* to grapple with her bereavement at the loss of her husband and then wrote a companion piece, *Blue Nights*, on the death of her daughter and its unbearable pain.

I raise this point—about making as a way to know the self—to suggest that, despite their reticence to speak in these terms, designers (like writers) are also necessarily engaged in the personal. The design process is different from that of the artist, to be sure, and many designers are quick to point that out. But I believe that the focus on the addition of a client—or such considerations as industry, profit, and production—can erroneously lead one to conclude that the designer's own personal engagement and private insights are somehow not part of the thing produced. It doesn't get talked about much in design circles, but great design does reflect the deeper sensibilities, values, convictions, and experiences of those who create it. To disassociate the personal from design is to miss the infusion of something all too human.

Great design, I would argue, will always have the personal inside of it, as part of it. Otherwise we might not be very interested in it. That designed thing, that object, carries a thoughtfulness and personal conviction that we may not understand or articulate clearly, or even recognize immediately in its final manifestation. But it somehow informs our attachment to the design and the quality we see in it. Make to know helps us understand how the personal enters design.

Paula Scher, an internationally celebrated designer, tells me about the "subconscious" discoveries that come through for her while sketching. "I'm starting something and it starts out sort of stiff and contrived from some pre-existing idea I have. And then in the doing and in the process, I see something." She goes on to specify that the process of discovery for her is a kind of personal defamiliarization; it is a way of knowing something she already holds by seeing it in a different context. Note the make-to-know orientation of her words: "There's a thing that becomes triggered from making, a discovery of knowledge I already had, through a new framework. As a designer, you're going to revisit many of the things you already know about scale in typography and messaging and all of that, but when the frame changes, when the frame is new, there's a mammoth discovery."

"And how do you, Paula, get to that new frame?" I ask.

"I explain it as a form of freefall, free play. You suspend your belief system and your set of tricks and what you think you know and don't know. You suspend it and you're in this state that you put yourself in, to subconsciously make a discovery. And for me it's usually through sketching."

Scher specifies that the "state of play" through which she find her ideas, her personal connection, happens in those "shower" or "driving" moments of discovery that we have already heard are common to other artists. "You need to be in a state of play, in a state of making or semi-paying attention to allow this sort of *subconscious* behavior to take place, to give you ideas." She goes on to describe more specifically what that state is like for her. "I thought I was more creative when I smoked—smoking was a break after I completed an activity. I may have been writing a letter and then stopped to have a cigarette. You can get a lot of ideas because you're not paying attention to anything specifically, except smoking. My problem is that I replaced smoking with reading my emails and that actually uses conscious energy. And I found that I lost a lot of my creative space that way. Because smoking and standing around is nothing; I mean nothing is going on, so *everything* is going on."

Scher offers a specific example from the day of our interview to demonstrate how she accesses her own thinking and how she enters the state of play, through sketching. On this particular occasion, however, she is under the constraints of a deadline which, in her words, changes the scene: "You can't just stand around bored and drooling to have a wonderful 'aha' moment." Nonetheless, she finds her way to creating openings and solutions through making. It allows her to know in that same defamiliarized, albeit more pressing, fresh context. "Just this afternoon, I had to find some solutions to a problem—and I did it the sketchbook way because that never fails. What inevitably works for me is just sketching my way into it." She specifies how it works: "If I'm designing something like a logo on a piece of paper, where I can't perfect it, it's frustrating because I think it always looks sloppy." She then finds her "mindless," "smoking-like" opening through the reflexive process of perfecting the necessarily imperfect work. That in itself brings her to a state of play crucial for discovery. The reflexive becomes "mindless" and the play toward discovery begins. "The mindless part is trying to make the thing that I think I'm drawing neat, and while I'm doing this mindless activity...that's where I make the discovery." In other words, the making in this instance is the reflexive activity of working the logo, which in turn for her becomes a state of play in itself that brings her own real and very personal solution to the fore. She knows it through this making.

Scher's point is a subtle one, and gives evidence of a seasoned designer who knows herself well. Her point about deliberately creating a state of play—or "mindlessness"—in order to access something of the self, how she thinks, crystallizes for me while I am interviewing designer Anne Burdick, who expresses a very similar notion but in a different context. "I doodle in meetings. That's a way for me to listen. It keeps a certain aspect of my brain occupied, which frees up the other one to be open. So it's kind of like, you know, driving or being in the shower, because I'm doing something that is rote."

Perfecting the logo. Doodling in a meeting. Smoking a cigarette. Repetitive gestures. All of these are part of make to know; all of these are part of solving problems.

BUILDING CONSTRAINTS
Designing can only come about within a field of constraints, both social and technical.
—POUL BITSCH OLSEN AND LORNA HEATON[9]

Models and prototypes are, on one level, ways of testing ideas and concepts. But there is another level on which they function, one that fewer of us recognize as part of the creative endeavor—that of incorporating constraints and finding limits.

We typically think of constraints in a negative sense, but designers tell me they are often able to use them in a way that is integral to the making itself. I am able to relate to this point as a theater director, knowing full well the extraordinary creative value of opening night, itself a built-in constraint of a production. What happens through the constraint and necessity of a deadline, of a show that will inevitably exist before an audience, is itself a reality of the making process. And it can, sometimes, seem to contain a kind of magic. I cannot quantify how many shows of mine were in states of total disarray during the final week of technical and dress rehearsals, only to find coherence and strength on opening night.

Constraints help to focus, to limit, to hone the creative imagination. There are practical constraints that are inherent to a project or brief—budget, schedule, and regulatory requirements, among others. Those too can help limit possibilities and focus a designer's attention. But more pertinent for our purposes is to recognize a more deliberate, creative element of constraint for designers—making through three-dimensional modeling and prototyping. Designers speak of this in many ways, the most common of which is in the language of "failing." Failing is a way to engender possibility, a way to find an idea.

Industrial designer Yves Behar talks about sketching as a way to get "all the bad ideas out of my brain." Frido Beisert similarly associates failing and prototyping as a way of moving toward a solution. He talks specifically about his appreciation for "fail-fast prototyping." He states quite emphatically that "making is the solution to everything. It's not always physical. I think prototyping can be digital. It can be anything."

Beisert also teaches at the international business school INSEAD. He offers an interesting distinction between the way his business and his design students think. "There's a fundamental difference in how we approach things, and it's fascinating to me. In the business school, I tell my students 'Here's the problem—go solve it.' And what they do is think through a Rolodex of case studies, of how someone else has solved the problem in the past, and they try to find the single best solution from that. They apply something that's been done before to solve the problem. Designers don't rely on existing things necessarily to solve problems." Beisert then concludes in language reminiscent of artist Ann Hamilton's deliberate cultivation of "not knowing." With that mindset, he believes designers can then work toward an answer through the narrowing of possibilities. "It's having the confidence," he says of designers, "of not knowing what the solution is and allowing that process of elimination to lead you to create something that is entirely new." Designers "eliminate" their way to a solution.

Interaction designer Maggie Hendrie expresses the issue this way: "I work in the world where people model things all the time. We make algorithms about how to drive down the street, algorithms about how to find true love, algorithms about how to find the home that your family will be happy in. We model it into an algorithm. And by their very nature, the models are reductive. That's the nature of the model. Exclusion and inclusion."

Michael Maltzan is, as we have seen, a prolific model maker, one who seeks a "physical declaration" of ideas. It is his only way to a design. He too will work with those models to discover what the project "is not" and go through a process of eliminating ideas. "I often find that those first physical forms don't carry my ambition in the way that I wanted it to. I often find that they're wrong, that they're off." He uses a variety of techniques and tools, everything from digital fabrication to hands-on making of models. It is a way for him to deal with an array of choices for a given project and to build some kind of limit around those choices. In that process of creating limits, he builds a framework that, paradoxically, he sees as the key to his "improvisational" process. "I think of it as a framework or armature that the improvisational process has to work within. You know where those terminal points are. You know what it feels like. You know where you have latitude and where you have less latitude, and I think the model allows you to live within the spaces of that framework more fluidly."

I cannot think of a better way than Maltzan's framework to illustrate that modeling and prototyping are, essentially and paradoxically, a narrowing that opens possibility. The framework, the parameters, the limits, allow for improvisation. It's often exactly the same in music and theater—improvisation cannot emerge out of nothing. There is a framework built through the elimination of *total* possibility that allows the maker(s) to get at *some* possibility. It is a context for discovery made through elimination. It is the prompt for theatrical improv. It is the melody on which the jazz musician builds a riff. It is the frame, the context, that entering uncertainty requires. It is different practically, but not fundamentally, from Amy Tan's cosmology or even Aimee Bender's physical tie to her chair. Limits, laws, and constraints are key to discovery.

DIGITAL PROTOTYPES

What are the implications of new technologies and the ways in which they function for the design process? I asked all of the artists and designers I spoke to about how they believed "digital making" might have changed the conversation. They replied by saying things like "Digital prototyping allows me to move more rapidly through ideas," or "It's a different context, and therefore I can see with fresh eyes," or "The materiality of the digital makes all the difference."

Maggie Hendrie is particularly eloquent on this topic. She sees modeling as something that "mimics understanding." For her, digital making allows for a different kind of modeling but, she is quick to suggest, it is also simply another canvas on which to create. She herself is a designer of digital tools that other creatives use, and so her perspective is thought-provoking. "When we are thinking in the digital world about whether you are designing for a mobile or screen or a physical environment, we call them canvases—which I think is interesting. I want to know how we design digital tools. The model is based on the designer's or artist's work process and their habits of mind."

In other words, a designer like Hendrie investigates first the habits and processes of creativity and allows that to inform the digital tools being built. She focuses on three major elements that the digital world affords—access, collaboration, and versioning—all of which enhance an already-existing process of making. "Anybody who has a laptop" has access "to the world of image making, video making, music making." And with the digital designers on teams, wherever they might be, they can collaborate in an instant. The ease of digital allows for making "multiple versions"—i.e., models to be tested, enhanced, or eliminated.

I tried to investigate virtual reality (VR) as a technology that might have significant implications for the making process. Imagine donning a VR headset and virtually stepping inside the designed model one has created for a building, a car, or an experience. When I spoke to Hendrie about this, she referenced acting theory and stage design. Her point was that interaction designers need to understand how people move through space: "stretching, reaching, touching, tapping, zooming, moving." This understanding makes them better designers for a VR experience; but how different is the process of getting there because of this technology? It's access, collaboration, and versioning. We may understand objects and movement in new ways through the framework of VR, but the fundamentals of making—sketching, modeling, prototyping, collaborating—do not seem to change.

Chapter 5

IMPROVISATIONAL MAKING: THE FLOW OF LIVE PERFORMANCE

*It is easier to act yourself into a new way of thinking,
than it is to think yourself into a new way of acting.*
—MILLARD FULLER[1]

*Begin by...free associating...until some patterns
emerge that begin to intrigue you solely for the
sound they make, their rustle of possibility.*
—DAVID MORLEY[2]

Live performance is always in motion. It is never fixed. A performance can be prepared, structured, rehearsed, and memorized. But because it occurs in real time and because it exists in a dynamic with an audience (no matter how large or small), the creation will vary, even in ways perhaps minute and imperceptible to a spectator. This principle of fundamental fluidity is essential to any exploration of the creative process for performers, and it provides another important context in which to study make to know. As actor Diego Matamoros states eloquently about the live acting process: "To me, it's about finding a flow, and then that flow, because it's liquid, will always be malleable and moveable with an audience, and so you're never thrown by an audience reaction, because you expect it." Making in flow, liquidity, malleability, movement, expecting the unexpected—these are some of the fundamental ingredients of make to know in the world of performance.

IMPROVISATIONAL MAKING

The purest manifestation of the fluid nature of performance is improvisation, itself a most effective way of illustrating the making/knowing relationship. By definition, one cannot know the product of improvisation until one improvises. The making of the invention and the invention itself are one and the same, and to brave the improvisational is to create a rich arena of discovery.

Think John Coltrane's saxophone solos, or Miles Davis's performance on an album like *Kind of Blue*. Davis knew the music only in the moment he played it on his trumpet, creating the album almost entirely on the first take. Keith Jarrett, at the Köln Concert of 1975, improvised a spectacular evening of piano music, and the recording of that night's work became a bestselling album. Neither the artist nor the audience could know the passion, beauty, and musical contours of Jarrett's work until he improvised, until he invented it in the moment. In fact, improvisation is often the source of much of the music we enjoy every day, no matter what the era or source of creation. As the late musician Jeff Pressing remarked, "In a large portion of the world's musical traditions, the composer and performer are not only one and the same, but the music is, to varying degrees, invented in the moment of performance."[3]

We do not often associate classical Western music with improvisation, but much of what emerged from medieval times to the Romantic era stems from a great tradition of improvising. Bach, Handel, Mozart: all were known for their improvisational work and for the freedom and agility of their impromptu playing. Beethoven, when he first arrived in Vienna, demonstrated great skill in improvisation and gained a reputation as an extemporaneous performer before finding fame as a composer. Frédéric Chopin and Franz Liszt were inveterate improvisers whose pieces often took form only on the instrument and in the moment. They needed to "play" in order to "know" the music they created.

Indian classical music also includes improvisational elements that are integral to its composition. The intention in this tradition is to ensure that the improvisational will always be an ongoing part of performance. The concept of the *raga* is a case in point. A *raga* is an array of varied melodic structures of several notes (at least five). It is a musical frame within which a performer can improvise both sequence and tone. Indian musicians see the *raga* (a word etymologically related to color or mood) as a way to evoke certain feelings in the listener, feelings symbolic of season, emotion, or time. But those feelings are always products of the moment, of the improvisation of the player. Knowing the feeling is only in the making.

FRAMES OF MUSICAL IMPROVISATION

The word "improvise" comes from the Latin *improviso* (unforeseen or unexpected), which is itself formed by the negative prefix *in-* and *provisus* (foreseen or provided). To improvise, then, is to enter the unforeseen and confront the unexpected—experiences which are, of course, central animating principles of this book. But what I have learned from conversations with improvisers (no matter the discipline) is that we often misunderstand that which is "provided" and that which is not. Much is left open, to be sure, but there are, in fact, requirements necessary for the making to emerge at all. Improvisation, and make to know generally, perhaps counterintuitively does not and cannot transpire without structure or context. Making the unforeseen necessitates some provision. Skill, discipline, and experience are all examples of those provisions. And a frame for improvising itself is perhaps one of the most significant requirements of all.

A frame can be many things—a musical structure (*raga*), a mood, a major or minor key, or even a tune like George Gershwin's "Summertime" that can serve as context for a Miles Davis solo melody. In a similar vein, the frame of theatrical improvisation can take the form of a situation, particulars of a moment in space and time, parameters of language and character, emotion, or engagement. Frames can come *before* the making (as in Gershwin's tune, or the particulars of a theatrical improv), or they can emerge *through* the making itself (as will become evident below). Frames differ from points of entry, not so much in terms of chronology (that which comes first), but in the way they function in the making. A point of entry is just that—an urge, a question, a physical presence—whereas a frame is the context and structure in which the making ensues. Both are essential to the improvisational process.

Pianist Francis Martineau, the multitalented teacher I mentioned in Chapter 1 whose work is improvisational at its core, explains the creation of his solo piano pieces in performance: "I sit down to play without having any clue as to what is going to come out. That is the way I prefer it. It was Keith Jarrett who said you have to empty yourself entirely before a concert so that you have absolutely no preconceptions at all in your beginning—and then it's wide open for you. As soon as you have a preconceived notion about where you're going to begin, it restricts it. And I totally go with that."

In Martineau's case the entry point is not a question, an idea, or even a mood—at least, not consciously. Instead, he "empties" himself as preparation for engaging with the piano in performance. Martineau clarifies, however, that even though he "empties" himself, "it doesn't mean to say that form is therefore wiped out." The distinction is subtle but enormously important. He begins without a notion, without knowing, and yet a structure, a frame, what he calls "form," emerges from the first instance of the making. Indeed, the frame comes *through* the playing. Martineau calls on himself as a listener to the "music-in-the-making" in order to detect that frame. In his words, "you have got to be hyper-aware as the material makes itself known to you."

"Hyper-aware as the material makes itself known to you," I repeat. "Is it possible to be even more specific about how that works for you?"

"As I'm playing, I am selecting things that I would like to return to in some way," Martineau clarifies. "It's about theme and variation, that kind of idea. It emerges in the playing but has a certain conscious element to it; I have to remember it, but I can't stop playing." Here we come to the beauty of what improvised music, in its time-based structure and performative context, can uncover. The playing reveals the music to the player and excites continued playing. "The music is evolving," Martineau says, "and as it happens, I need to be very attentive to what I think has more quality in it."

"You hook onto something?"

"Exactly. I hook onto something, but I have no idea what it is going to be at the outset. I have to be aware as I'm playing of what I think is the most attractive thing that I've created so far."

"And is it attractive because it stirs something in you?"

"It's attractive because it's beautiful. It simply has a beauty to it that is greater than anything I've played up to that moment." Martineau holds on to that beauty. He remembers it as he plays. He elaborates on it and finds variation in it. In the end, his process involves a delicate balance of spontaneity, memory, openness to create form. "It's all in the moment. It's purely memory working in your favor to make music as you play, give it a form, and help you concentrate on the best of what you're playing." The improvising artist creates a frame on the fly.

Contrast Martineau's description of his experience with the reflections of award-winning musician Kurt Swinghammer. He talks to me about his involvement in an ensemble called Faceless Forces of Bigness (FFoB), a self-described "electronic collective" that, for almost twenty years, has "explored generative composition within the parameters of real time improvisation."

At first, when Swinghammer tells me about his experience, it sounds very much like Martineau's. "There is no preconceived idea of what we are going to come up with. It's an example of just trusting your instincts and making decisions based on what you are responding to. I hear something, and I have no way of knowing what's going to come next, but I respond. You can only respond and manipulate to try to make the sound beautiful." He plays with the FFoB ensemble maybe once a year, so there's no familiarity that guides the outcome. The infrequency "keeps it completely fresh, and there are not enough opportunities for us to settle into patterns. I think that's when the real magic happens, when you don't know what's going to occur and you're not relying on muscle memory and familiar chord changes and getting into patterns of repeating yourself."

When I ask Swinghammer about the emergence of a frame, he balks at first and veers on this point from Martineau. "It doesn't have any frame, really, because there are no chord changes that give you the information of what to work on in terms of scales and things." He contrasts the work with jazz, in which he does recognize far more structure. "A lot of jazz is really coming out of the academic formal traditions where they know exactly the chord changes in every note that is played." With FFoB, Swinghammer engages in a process dubbed "free improvisation." "Free because there are no chords pinning you down," he says. "It's easy to get into a cacophony and just a big pile of mess."

Swinghammer's experience with "free improv," he tells me, is also relevant to another collective he played with for many years called CCMC, led by the visual artist and musician Michael Snow. The band describes itself as "a free music orchestra devoted to spontaneous composition." The literature of this ensemble specifies that point in the following statement: "CCMC are as comfortable playing toys and melodies as they are noise electronics and torrential freak-outs. In the truest sense, CCMC are sonic explorers devoted to spontaneous free music, uninhibited by any restriction, be it melody, silence, genre, volume or instrumentation."[4]

Do "sonic explorers" and creators of "music uninhibited by any restriction" still operate in some kind of frame? The extreme nature of so-called "free improvisation" provides an instructive context in which to explore the question, and Swinghammer references two particular thoughts that help address it.

The first is evident in his reflection that CCMC, in its sonic explorations, produces "sounds that are *textural*," and the second has to do with the ensemble and the need to engage with others to make the music. What emerges from my conversation with Swinghammer is that this kind of improvising does not generally take the form of capturing "beautiful themes" like a piano solo by Martineau. And yet it produces something equivalent as far as a frame for improvisation is concerned: "texture," a quality at least partially resulting from its heavy electronic sound. This collective improvising, moreover, also produces a necessary frame of "action and response" among members of a group. Two frames operate simultaneously that make improvising possible. Sonic materiality (texture) creates the first frame, as loose as it may be. The artist engages with that material, not unlike Ann Hamilton engaging (and improvising) space, or Martineau with beauty. And the texture itself, functioning like a melody or theme, then becomes a core element of a frame for additional making and play. Working with an ensemble necessarily requires structural framing to enable a collective process. It's impossible to imagine collaborative making without it. As Swinghammer concludes, "We are basically curating our palette as individuals in the collective in a way that, together, our intentions make something—something that sounds like music."

Textural sound, coordinated performance, live engagement with an audience, response to multiple circumstances—all, even in a seemingly "free" making, comprise creative structure. They exemplify the kinds of things that can constitute the "provision" of improvisation, which is necessary to the making.

Swinghammer makes a further point about the making of these improvisational sonic creations; he speaks of a kind of discipline, a deliberate openness to spontaneity (not unlike that which we saw in Diana Thater's installation art and film work in Chapter 2). For the musician, that discipline, that state of readiness and receptivity, advances a way to discovery. "I do recognize that it's kind of a zone where I'm allowing something magical to happen. It's like in life when amazing coincidences happen, things you don't anticipate. You have to be ready and allow them to happen. You have to step back in order not to intervene in things that might prevent them from happening. It's always felt a bit spiritual, a magical place to be. It's letting energy manifest itself. It sounds a little corny, and I don't really have that side of my life in other areas, but in performance it feels a bit shamanistic." In the context of this chapter, that very state of readiness is, for the artist, yet another frame of making, and one that operates on a deeply personal level through improvised performance.

It might seem or "feel" as if one can enter the making process free of all structure, but there exists always a discipline together with building blocks or a kind of fundamental grammar with which the artist works— words, images, sounds, notes, materials, and collaborative rules. As makers, we default to structure. We organize into categories. We thrive on markers and groupings and organizational patterns. The structural elements of the frame emerge for some artists with deep intention. For others, like Amy Tan and Francis Martineau, they manifest through the making itself. Even in the most open and free processes—including free association, free improvisation, or stream-of-consciousness writing—we always *make* in some kind of frame, wide or narrow.

FRAMES OF THEATRICAL IMPROVISATION

Actor and director Paolo Santalucia directed an improvised show, *Entrances and Exits*, in the summer of 2018. This project is a stimulating example of what theatrical improvisation can uncover about make to know—not least that "directing" improvisation essentially involves creating a frame for spontaneous performance. "I really only gave suggestions on some formal things," Santalucia tells me. "And besides, improvisers don't want to rehearse." These comments are, in themselves, interesting and deserve attention. But first, we need some specifics about *Entrances and Exits* itself.

"It's based on a farce," he explains. "The first twenty minutes take place in a living room. An emcee character asks the audience for a reason that a group of people would get together. They also ask them for three sounds that they would never want to hear coming out of an adjacent bedroom at such a gathering. There's a couch on the stage and a door that leads to the bedroom. The first act is improvising the get-together in the living room.

"The action then changes to the bedroom. The couch is a pullout and turns into the bed. They do the whole thing again from the top, but this time the audience sees it from what was previously offstage space. It's all improvised. The group I worked with was extraordinary." He pauses to confess, "You know, sometimes the piece didn't work at all." He takes a beat, energy shifts, and then he says with excitement, "But when it did come together, it was amazing."[5]

Several thoughts surface quite quickly in my conversation with Santalucia that illuminate the various frames operative in this kind of improvisational work. I am intrigued, first off, by his observation of his actors' resistance to rehearsing and to anything that might counter the spontaneity of actual performance. Performers, like so

Cast of *Entrances and Exits*, directed by Paolo Santalucia, 2018.

many of the other artists and designers I've spoken with, tend to resist anything that might "fix" their work or cause them to rely on the habitual. They rightly caution against the perils of the set routine. On the other hand, Santalucia understands that a frame is still a necessary "provision." The director's work in this context isn't about setting anything, but about helping actors find a structure to create the unforeseen. Again, there is a generative relationship between structure and spontaneity.

Consider, for example, the situational frame Santalucia developed with respect to the get-together in the living room and the activities in the bedroom. When I ask him how this situational frame functioned, he refers to "constraints," a notion I discussed in the last chapter as a catalyst for making. The same principle operates in a theatrical context. The improvisation works partly because, in the director's words, "the actors knew what they were going to be playing into and that came from setting constraints." Santalucia sets rules to open the improvisational. "These rules give everyone the freedom to perform in big ways because they know what it is they are responsible for." Rules and constraints spur the creative enterprise. Listening to Santalucia, I reflect back on the seeming absence of rules in Swinghammer's "free improv" experiences. It strikes me that Santalucia's statement gives us another way to recognize the functioning of frames in a musical context. In other words, musical free improv ensembles can operate only through some rules of exchange in live performance; the sounds emerge through constraints of texture, and that guides the emergence of the music. Rules and constraints serve as the material of frames.

The situational context of living room and bedroom in Santalucia's piece establishes as well a dynamic of perspective that gives evidence of another frame operating in the mix. As the second scene follows on the first, the performance establishes a functional layering. The bedroom action is always tied to what occurred first in the living room and will always create a constraint on that second scene. It is a reality the performers need to bring to their making consciousness. The interchange is not unlike Martineau's remembering the "beautiful theme" he hooks onto and wishes to bring back, through memory and in variation, even as he plays. The improvisers of this dramatic piece must similarly carry memory of the first scene as they improvise the second. The audience itself mirrors this dynamic in the viewing, in the oscillation of direct experience of one scene and the recollection of the other. For the performers, the combination of real-time making and memory constitutes a frame of working. Fluid performance that is at the same time structurally bound defines the make to know of live theater.

Another significant frame operates through the participation of the audience, who generate ideas at the outset and become partners in the making. In this way, *Entrances and Exits* employs a rather clever strategy. Assuming there are no spectator plants (in which case, it wouldn't be much of an improvisation), the audience members, through their suggestions, are a direct part of the process of setting up a frame. As such, they are collaborators, and their creative involvement narrows the gap between the roles of observer and observed. Implied is a tacit honesty of—and in—the work. From the audience perspective, offering ideas previously unknown to the performers guarantees that the spectators are about to see something genuinely improvised. It establishes an assurance that the actors are creating in the moment, even within a predetermined context. Involved spectators will drop their suspicion of something having been rehearsed and planned so that they might find amazement in spontaneity. From the actor's perspective, on the other hand, the work unfolds in honest connection with an audience that believes in the authenticity of all that is before them. For the actor, that positive dynamic with the spectator affects the quality of work—something that many of the performers I talk to mention in conversation. Two frames (at least) are thus operating simultaneously: the frame of situation and the frame of collaboration. Actor and spectator participate in both.

Finally, as Santalucia makes clear, "sometimes it [the show] doesn't work." I think this is a vital point. The artists and designers discussed in earlier chapters never face a live audience in the same way that these actors do. But like those artists and designers, the actors in improvisation sometimes fail. This is a natural part of make to know. The failure will manifest in a performance that falls flat because an ensemble miscommunicates, or because of an actor's poor choice, or for whatever reason the theater gods might have. On the one hand, the failure itself can feel terrible. But on the other hand, the very risk of failure gives the performance an energy and life it could never have if it were fixed. I'm not suggesting that well-rehearsed and prepared productions lack spontaneity or the potential for failure. They do contain those elements, and that spontaneity is always an energizing force of live theater. The point, however, is that risk is the stuff of improvisation, its sustenance. There is a potential for breakdown at any moment, and that danger yields a special energy to the performance. Improvisation is in many ways a crystallization of the make-to-know process, with its potential for both great success and utter failure. It is dramatic, exciting, and fertile ground for discovering that which would otherwise be impossible to find.

THE KNOWING IS IN THE BODY

I had the opportunity to discuss improvisation in a very specific context with Leah Cherniak, an actor, director, and teacher who studied "clown" at L'Ecole Internationale de Théâtre Jacques Lecoq in Paris. Jacques Lecoq (1921–1999), who founded the school, was a French actor and mime who taught a very specific physical approach to performance. What intrigues me particularly when I interview Cherniak, however, is the way the Lecoq School uses masks in its training program to support improvisational making and discovery. One operative principle, as she explains, holds that by deactivating both facial expression and speech the body is set free to express and improvise most fully.

"At first, the Lecoq approach does not include words," Cherniak says. "Lecoq was always interested in universal gesture which, you know, is contentious today—can there be such a thing? I think I eventually knew what he meant in terms of a search for what a universal gesture might be and then how it varies from one culture to another. It's a great starting point to explore a potential universality in the human condition, which is what he was always searching for. And it's generally found in the body and not necessarily with words."

The performer at the Lecoq School would don a "neutral mask," which, Cherniak explains, is "intended as a way to expand physical potential." She quickly articulates appropriate reservation about the term "neutral": "Neutral is a bit misleading because neutral is not nothing." This corrective is illuminating, with echoes of Hamilton's "responsive place": "It's actually creating a state of hyper-availability." The mask brings the performer to a state of readiness, an "availability" of what the body might know.

"Are these improvisational techniques?" I ask her.

"Yes, they are. But I need to clarify. For Lecoq, they were mainly training techniques. They were tools to train an actor, to train a creative being, to train a maker of creative pieces or characters. The more you train that way, the more it becomes second nature for your body to become a conduit of making."

I understand the distinction between training and actual performance in this context. But the fundamental point about the consequence

Example of neutral mask originally created in 1958 for Jacques Lecoq by Italian sculptor and poet Amleto Sartori.

of suppressing face and voice is really what interests me here. The great French teacher invented a practice to find the depths of one form of expression by reducing others. The discovery of what the body knows emerges through elimination of that which might impede its fullest expression. The "neutralizing" of one element engenders creative opportunity through another.

"I think when you can't explain what you're doing through your face or words," Cherniak continues, "when you take away the tools that you've become so accustomed to using for expression, when you suddenly don't have that, you access something else and, most of the time, you become quite astonished by what comes out of your body." The neutral mask sets up a context, and a frame, for physical improvisation.

The great Polish director Jerzy Grotowski, in his 1968 book *Towards a Poor Theatre*, offers a specific term to describe the idea of finding expression through elimination: "Via Negativa," a concept that Lecoq himself consciously adopted. Grotowski's interest was in finding an "essential theatre," one devoid of anything extraneous: "The acceptance of poverty in theatre, stripped of all that is not essential to it, revealed to us not only the backbone of the medium, but also the deep riches which lie in the very nature of the art-form."[6]

This same attempt to find the essential, the "riches" that come from "stripping away," is evident specifically in the performer's work through the Via Negativa. As Grotowski makes clear, Via Negativa is "not a collection of skills, but an eradication of blocks."[7] What Lecoq and Grotowski teach is a way to consider a making/knowing relationship that emerges from the removal of obstacles, a process of subtraction that enables expression. In my own experience, I recall a singing teacher I had at Stanford University who held fast to this very same philosophy about singing. She believed with deep conviction that singing was about removing that which blocked the voice from coming through. Her teaching set the voice free by eliminating both the physical and emotional impediments that restrict it.

The "eradication of blocks" was, for Grotowski, a make-to-know strategy that he explained in temporal terms relevant to improvisation. His technique was designed to short-circuit time; he wanted the performer "to achieve a freedom from the time-lapse between inner impulse and outer reaction," when "impulse and action are concurrent." He thought about creativity as physical reflex and not intellectual discovery. It is thinking with the body that he likened to moments of surprised astonishment. He sought in the performer the reflexive expression that comes at a moment of "psychic shock, a moment of terror, of mortal danger or tremendous joy."[8] Grotowski (and Lecoq) offered ways of making that reveal what the body and its reflexes might know.

I would add, however, that it is not much of a leap to extrapolate ideas like the Via Negativa or the neutral mask to other creative disciplines as well. I am thinking of Rebeca Méndez talking about "removing the filters" of perception in her process of making art and design, of Ann Hamilton cultivating "not knowing" when approaching an installation piece, and of Martineau (and Jarrett) "emptying" as a way toward musical invention. It strikes me all as one and the same.

A fascinating postscript I want to add came from my conversation about the neutral mask with Cherniak. I was curious about the outward-facing nature of a mask. One would think that the "neutralizing" would affect the perceiver and not the performer. Why would the latter experience the change?

"Because you actually feel it," she tells me. "You feel this power of the mask on your face. You look at it, you touch it, you feel it and put it on. And you also know the rules. And the main rule is: *You're trying to find the right body to wear this mask.*" For Lecoq, the body holds the key to a lot of information that we are not generally using, especially as creators and makers. "Knowing is such a heady term," Cherniak contends. "When I hear it, I immediately go to an intellectual process. But it's not. The knowing is in the body."

And then, most curious of all, Cherniak asserts, "You enter another state with that mask. And I have seen, when people take off the mask, when Lecoq or the teacher would take off the mask at the end, their faces would look so different. So, so different. It is as if they were in some weird state. It's transformative."

Following the learning that might come with the neutral mask, the actor moves on in Lecoq's world to using character masks with much greater specificity, masks expressive of certain emotions: happy or sad, confused, delighted, playful, mad, lustful. As Cherniak makes clear, the performer's capacity to access the body through work with the neutral mask is a developed skill. The shift to masks that denote more specific characteristics and emotions continues the trajectory. Now the face/mask emerges as an active element.

According to Cherniak, one can understand this next level of making through one of the smallest character masks of the repertoire, the clown's red nose. For her, the nose is both catalyst and context for something very personal to come through. "The clown nose is a mask that asks you to harness a part of yourself that may make you both vulnerable and strong at the same time. That red nose is an internal place of being, a human place of being." As such, she tells me, it leads her into the improvisational, to a place of honesty, to the humor of the clown born of that honesty in a frame of vulnerability and strength.

Cherniak describes teaching actors about the potential of the red nose. "One of the first exercises is to stand, without the nose on, in front of an audience. You look at the audience and say your name. And then you go away. That's a first level of being seen. It causes you to go to a different place inside, a less defensible place. Then you put the nose on and you stand in front of the audience, and you are instructed to do nothing but look at them and be looked at. Sometimes people laugh, sometimes they cry, sometimes they close down. It's important just to try to keep yourself in the experience, to recognize there's an energy going between you and the audience. There's something about that little nose that strips something away, that makes you feel, perhaps, a little ridiculous, a little bit seen—really seen—all from this tiny red mask, this red round mask."

Cherniak contends that the performer's job, with red nose affixed, is then to improvise to know the character of the clown that will evolve. "You have to start by getting to know your clown—what is this clown, who is this person? And it will always be some extension of who you are. You funnel yourself through this nose, and you are very aware that you look different and that you might not look as strong as you might want to be. You use the nose to build up this little creature. You improvise. You don't really know the character until you've made it."

The clown nose may be a completely foreign element to most people and something that no one would ever dream could be a way to frame creative expression or to learn about the self. But it obviously holds a power. "It changes how you operate in the world," Cherniak reveals, "even for just a short time, or for a longer time, or forever, depending on how much it gets inside of you. For me it's because the experience is inside the body, and that's why it is so transformative." All through a little red nose.

IMPROVISING CHARACTER

The clown nose and its function as a frame for improvising character suggest interesting comparisons to the actor working with a role already written through text. How does the actor enter and frame the development of a performance of a written character? I should say from the outset that there are myriad acting styles, theories, and definitions. My approach here is simply to reflect my conversations and to extrapolate some clear principles of how actors might use improvisation to know character and to articulate their ideas behind the make to know of performance.

For award-winning actor Michael Laskin, the way into a character for theater all begins with the text. Interestingly, this is an actor whose work with text is a variation on how a clown might use the red nose. "Once I know the text, and it becomes second nature, I can start to fill it out in a way that's more emotional and character-driven. But I have to know the text first. My process is much more outside-in, by instinct."

Laskin goes on to describe an experience he had while studying at Northwestern University. There was a moment in which he discovered a costume that gave him a frame (*before* the making) for a character he was playing, an experience that reinforced his "outside-in" orientation. "I put on this coat, and I looked in the mirror and said, 'Oh, yeah. Okay. That's him.' And that was kind of an 'a-ha moment' for me. Here were all these people tearing themselves inside out, dredging up horrible psychological slights of their childhood; and I just put on a coat and thought, 'Okay, that makes sense.'"

"And then it goes inside of you?" I ask.

"It totally goes inside. How I wear it changes how I walk—for me, it affects everything. It's just instinctively how I work. I work from externals." After that, the improvisational work can happen.

Actor Raquel Duffy, by contrast, explains to me that she very deliberately does not begin with learning her lines. She views early memorization as a possible restriction of her work. In a way, she empties herself in preparation. "I don't like to come in with my lines memorized beforehand just because I might rely on a preconceived way of saying things or with a preconceived notion of how I think the scene should go." She is also concerned that early focus on her lines makes the initial rehearsals too much about memorization and not sufficiently about what she needs to discover in the moment. "I don't really listen to what the other person is saying to me because I'm too worried about my next line."

Duffy is one of those artists who actually needs to cultivate a space of not knowing. "I think that making, whatever that making is for me, has to come from a place of 'I don't know.' I only have questions and the more I come from that place the more I can feel a sense of flow. The process of questioning and coming at the work without answers ends up being the most valuable to me." Duffy's frame emerges *through* the making.

Intriguingly, Duffy enters the rehearsal room and begins to engage not so much intellectually but on a spatial and physical level. "It's about what feels right in my body in relationship to the other actors or where I am onstage in the room." And she is very clear about when things feel right and when they do not. "It's a feeling. It's a sensory experience, nothing I know in my head. It just feels right." For Duffy, the making of the character in rehearsal is accessing what the body knows, discovering through physicality, through movement in space. Laskin moves to know a role from the external; Duffy through the body in space.

And curiously, Duffy is careful not to let anything too specific solidify in those early rehearsals. Her making at the beginning stage requires a commitment to staying open, to keeping the questions alive, to ensuring flexibility and experimentation, improvisation. "I don't want anything specific because it will lock. I feel like it will just lock me in too early to something." She talks about the great feeling of surprise that stems from staying open. "It comes out of nowhere. It is nothing that was preconceived but finding that surprise feels good. It's often not what I plan or what I thought about trying in rehearsal."

As our conversation continues, Duffy assimilates a variety of elements in the description of her process. Isolated moments begin to take shape through rehearsal, blocking and movement patterns evolve, and eventually she has a sense of what, in her words, is some kind of "outline or map of the journey of the character that I'm creating—and what everyone else is creating." They set up further constraints and function as the frame of her work.

She cites the first run-through of the play as a key moment of discovery. "I begin to get to know the piece. That first run-through isn't the best. But it's when I learn the journey of the character." It is rough, she says, but also another way in, finding rhythm, that first draft, with its brokenness and imperfection, prompting "revision" or, as we learn from writers, the next remaking. The first run-through is another frame, tighter than what precedes it and a context for further making, further improvisation. To use the language of design, it is a modeling phase and, as such, a building of definition. It is a narrowing that paradoxically opens further possibility for depth in the next iteration of making. Like Martineau, Duffy in a run-through needs to be "hyper-aware as the material makes itself known [to her]" and as it happens in real time. "You're just in the moment, going from moment to moment, and you have to surrender to that, learn from that. You have to give over to it. You can't stop because something doesn't work. If you do, you miss what's coming next."

With the learning of the run-through, the actor goes back to the text and to moments that are not working, places where she is stuck. And she engages with those moments, either on her own or with her fellow actors. They improvise ideas and play with things physically, emotionally, practically, psychologically. Revisiting moments of the text, I should emphasize, isn't always about analysis of what it means or what the sentences are or even what one is doing at a particular moment. It's work that is improvisational in nature and that helps the actor listen and engage with another part of herself.

Duffy continues: "I've done this work called imaging that I find really helpful. I just look at the text, take one word, and I inform that word not necessarily with the feeling, but with a color or an image. It doesn't have anything to do with the meaning of the sentence. It helps me to connect personally through images, to create a more personal relationship to some of the text." It's another part of the making process, one that circumvents the intellectual. The specificity of the image is not necessarily long-lasting. "Whatever those images are early on, you just throw them out, you never think about them again. I might use a color. It could be blue. It may or may not stick with me. But it might lead me somewhere else that is very fruitful."

There is another aspect of Duffy's process that is important to articulate here and that is a fundamental part of making in the theater. It is evident in her insistence on how she comes to know in relationship to the space of the performance, in the dynamic she has with one or more of the other characters, and even in the context of the first run-through. It is the reality and beauty of the individual's process of creating in the larger context of the theatrical experience, another frame of improvising and making. Specifically, the actor is part of a greater whole, a context of activity called the production, and exists in relationship to a complex network of things including, in the end, an audience. Diego Matamoros is particularly persuasive on this point and on the centrality of "actor making" in the context of what he calls "the event."

"Many actors begin by thinking, working on character, figuring out the background of a character, their education, where they come from—all the Stanislavski things to get background." But for Matamoros, that kind of study cannot happen in isolation because it fails to encompass the reality of the actor in the event. The theatrical event contains multiple elements on the stage at once: multiple voices (playwright, director, actor, character, and so on) as well as multiple questions, issues, ideas. His is an interest in how the actor participates or, in his words, "serves the event." Individual and separate preparation of character is contrary to theater's fundamental multiplicity. "You are within a reality, or a created reality, that is the event. You have to fit into that event along with others. The event, to me, is what has to rise up. It is what we need to communicate to the audience. As such, the artist is involved not only internally, but externally, in the environment, in the time progression of the whole thing." And it is in that context that Matamoros understands make to know in the creation of a role. Without the context of the event (another clear frame), the full making cannot happen. One cannot "know," therefore, until one enters that world.

Matamoros probes the internal/external dynamic more specifically. For this actor, the character, the text, the particularities of the role come as foreign matter. "You're given this thing to say. It's imposed on you until you figure out why it is that you say that particular thing and nothing else. At first it doesn't make sense. You try different ways to unlock the door to the thought or action—I'm talking about that which begins way before the text."

He cites Shakespeare's *Romeo and Juliet* as an example. "Is honor the bottom line?" For some characters in the play, he explains, "losing honor is losing themselves." For others, it is very different. "It is the difference between Romeo and Juliet, the characters, and the rest of the society they are in. The society is honor-bound, whereas Romeo and Juliet are love-bound. So there's a problem, because the bottom lines are different. Romeo and Juliet do not care about honor, they are going to do whatever they need to do in service of love. That creates the problem."

Matamoros certainly offers an interesting insight into a central dynamic of Shakespeare's play. But what I want to stress here is not so much the critical analysis of the text, but the process that happens for this actor in the development of a role. Once the actors begin to understand the differing "bottom lines," they then understand their characters in context of the larger whole. "You have to see that in a play—it's what I mean by the event. You have to understand and define the event. You get a sense of what you're living in, and a sense of what you're thinking in." In that way, we understand the personal work, the individual making, in a frame of creativity: this time not a Gershwin melody, or a retrieval of a spontaneous and beautiful passage, or the outlines of a situation, but of the world of the play itself, a world that the actor must engage with in the making of the character. And that world grows larger as the making of the whole evolves to incorporate the arc of the piece, the setting, the multiple dynamics of costume and lighting and movement and speech and audience.

"It all happens over time. You can't do it quickly. If you rush it you will only come up with fake solutions, not real solutions. It's not about failure or success. It's about finding the sense of things. There's a theater sense to the scene. There's a theater reality that gets established and that the audience can ride on."

IMPROVISING THEATRICAL COMPOSITION

Mouthpiece is a performance piece created and performed by Norah Sadava and Amy Nostbakken of the Toronto-based Quote Unquote Collective, a troupe that they founded as a way to "work outside the boundaries of tradition and expectation." The play is built fully on improvisation about a character named Cassandra (mythically conjuring the quintessential image of "woman ignored") who is desperately trying to find her voice as she wrestles with writing a eulogy for her mother's funeral. Both women play Cassandra simultaneously, performing various and competing parts of the character, speaking, searching, struggling—through text, music, and dance. The rich and layered meanings of the term "mouthpiece"—of speaking for another, of eulogy-making, of bit or bridle that imposes direction, of controlling what might be said—are remarkable and provocative.

The show premiered in Toronto in 2015, then toured throughout Europe and North America in 2017 (winning awards at the Edinburgh Festival Fringe) and through Canada and the United States in 2019. Film director Patricia Rozema also worked with Nostbakken and Sadava to create a film version of *Mouthpiece* that premiered at the Toronto International Film Festival in the fall of 2018.

Nostbakken is a graduate of the Lecoq School and approaches her work in the same spirit of physical improvisation described earlier by Leah Cherniak. When I talk with her about the creation of the play, the story reveals elements of make to know at once familiar and unique to this kind of work.

On the familiar side, Nostbakken and Sadava began their process with an agreement to show up, physically, with nothing planned, in a space in which they would write together and explore ideas that surfaced through their interaction. As is now recognizable, they were entering uncertainty and devising ways to find an entry point. They had, initially, a notion to develop something about female relationships. As they worked, they experienced many moments of feeling aimless and frustrated. Yet they persisted. "We would talk a lot," Nostbakken told me. "We would spend a lot of time exploring our own lives and thinking all the while 'this is a waste of time, we're wasting time.' But

Mouthpiece, created and performed by Norah Sadava and Amy Nostbakken of the Toronto-based Quote Unquote Collective, 2015.

we needed to be in a room for eight hours a day. We were frustrated. It was frustrating. Devising is frustrating."

The two artists were particularly resistant at first to creating a "feminist show." That label didn't resonate, at least in the moment, with who they were or what they wanted to explore. They were adamant (and perhaps protesting too much). "This isn't a feminist show," they would repeatedly insist to one another. "And if we call it a feminist show, nobody is going to come." Nostbakken goes on to conclude: "We weren't ready. We just weren't ready. But then three things happened."

I have recounted the experience of several artists and designers who sketch and write and *make* their way to discovery; and I have pointed out that sometimes, in a different space or context—often in the shower—a breakthrough occurs. In the case of *Mouthpiece*, Nostbakken had a series of experiences outside of the rehearsal hall that seemed to conspire around a direction for the show.

The first was her Facebook discovery of the birthday anniversary of the late Simone de Beauvoir. This inspired her to read some of de Beauvoir's work from decades ago. "And as I was reading, I thought it was so bang on. So current. So relevant." A few days after that, Nostbakken's cousin sent her an article about ads from the sixties and seventies and their depiction of women. "The article was pointing out how sick all of these ads were. Meanwhile I'm reading this on my laptop and the pop-up ads of today are around it. It was weird, so strange to witness the contemporary version of the very thing the article was critiquing." The third moment occurred when she happened upon the 1994 animated film *Thumbelina*. "I used to watch with my little sister. And I thought, I'll just watch a clip. I remember the music of it. And I ended up watching the whole thing and it struck me, 'this is pornography.'"

"All these revelations are nothing new," she continues. "But those three things in a row led to an 'a-ha moment': we're hypocrites."

In their introduction to the published play, Nostbakken and Sadava write: "As we explored the core of how women relate to one another, questioning how we define ourselves as women, talking about our lives in relation to our mothers and our mothers' mothers, one truth slapped us hard: we haven't changed as much as we would like to think."[9]

Nostbakken is clear in our conversation: "Of course, this is a feminist show. Of course, this show has to be about how we swallow the pill, about how I thought I was a free, liberated, progressive woman. We need to face our hypocrisies, reveal all of our secrets—like that moment I remember when I am in the shower alone, looking at my naked body. I actually imagine men seeing through my eyeballs, looking at my own body. I did that. It's inside of my eyeballs, in my eyelids. The patriarchy is built into me. And we need to talk about that. We haven't come as far as we think we have. The show had to address the dilemma."

It's a formidable task to set as an ambition revealing hypocrisy and "all our secrets." But that is what these collaborators did. It is stirring to hear Nostbakken speak about her process and to learn of the capacity of these artists to come through with courage and honesty. They developed a specific practice to move the project forward. They would sit and then respond to certain provocations—personal confessions or secrets. They would then separately write for twenty minutes, return and read to each other. They would build scenes from the writing, finding places of connection and depth. A show that had initially set out to explore female relationships was now something raw and open on a personal level. "We realized that in order to make a play about two women, we had to look at what a woman is. And what better research tool than to look inside? And once we started looking inside, all the confessions came out. The honesty came out."

Nostbakken compares her creative relationship with Sadava to a "jazz improvisation...It's all about listening carefully to each other." As Swinghammer also made clear, the ensemble of improvisation is one of trust and listening.

Nostbakken explains, "The content generation for this show had three dimensions to it: writing, music, and choreography. Lots and lots of writing. And then a bunch of compositions I created. I wanted the musical narrative to include a condensed history of female voices and music. So I would make a Billie Holiday composition or a Janis Joplin one or Joni Mitchell or a Bulgarian chant or a hymn or whatever. We then brought our choreography in and built movement pieces, music pieces, and text pieces." With this content, and with the material generated, they would then begin to improvise and play. Through that improvisation, they discovered how the various pieces fit together, tested the relationship of text and music, integrated the choreography. "So you have all this content and then you edit/direct the piece. In every scene, we asked which mode of communication—text, music, or movement—was the best way to express the moment."

In the end, a remarkable piece of theater surfaced, one they knew only through the very deliberate process of making it. The knowing of the theater piece was matched by a deeper knowing of the self—the process of making can give access to our deepest thoughts and feelings. As Nostbakken and Sadava write eloquently: "The play is a naked, vulnerable, raw set of truths that we have been terrified to expose, and that we have been completely liberated by. The writing, creation, and performance of *Mouthpiece* has changed us both as artists, as activists, and as women."

"*Mouthpiece*," Nostbakken concludes in our conversation, "took three years to develop. We had extreme doubts right up to the first preview. We were about to do a dress rehearsal and we both had the same thought—oh my God, maybe this is ridiculous. It's two women in white bathing suits running around, doing voices. But we just kept going. We were so terrified because it was so confessional. We just felt so naked."

Happily, it worked!

SINGER-SONGWRITERS

When I interview Dave Bidini, guitarist and original member of the Canadian indie rock band Rheostatics, he makes an intriguing comment: "On occasion, some songs will simply arrive more or less fully formed."

I press him on what he means, and he says that sometimes "a melody will just find me." In fact, several of the musicians interviewed for this book, especially singer-songwriters, echo Bidini's observation with some form of the following: "Once in a while, I just hear the melody in my head."

I wonder if this declaration is an indication that, with the exception of inveterate improvisers like Miles Davis, musicians work in a different way from the majority of artists and designers I've interviewed. Do

Canadian indie rock band Rheostatics, formed in 1978.

these artists know *before* they make? Is creating music the exception? Is there something about the experience of sound and of hearing that emerges from a distinct part of us, or that we are aware of in a special way? Perhaps songwriters operate more like Michelangelo. Perhaps they hear as he saw, with a clear knowledge of what is to come. Perhaps, like the Master, they manifest what they already know and set angels free from the marble of their internal music.

To an extent, I think musicians *are* different and that their creativity *does* have its own rules of development, including some form of working with internal sound. Acoustic cognition is a relatively new focus of neuroscientific study, and work in this area may help to improve our understanding of the creative process of musicians. But the more I've pressed artists who write songs, the more I've learned that even for those who first hear a melody "in their head," they still typically engage a make-to-know process. True, sometimes the song comes out perfectly (Paul McCartney famously dreamed "Yesterday" and then just wrote it down), but it's rare for that to happen.

It bears repeating that among the many artists and designers I've interviewed, some did reveal that occasionally vision precedes making and that the creative process can be about manifesting that vision. Songwriters are similar in this regard, but it seems to me that they have this experience more frequently. In the end, however, I believe that for musicians, particularly singer-songwriters, the difference in creative process is more practical than it is fundamental. Three distinct principles emerged in my conversations that persuaded me: 1) Singer-songwriters have unique entry points of discovery that can spark the writing and spur the formulation of the music (even in their heads); 2) Improvisation is typically a part of the process of creating a song, and core to its making; 3) Performance is the differentiator and a critical factor of creating a song.

My focus here is entirely on musicians who write songs and perform them live. The dynamic among these three forms of making a song—writing, improvisation, and live performance—is a rich and fascinating one. I do not cover musical composition generally or even the experience of these singer-songwriters with studio recording; these are issues of great interest, but they're beyond the scope of what I've explored in the interviews.

ENTRY POINTS FOR SONGWRITERS

My conversations with songwriters have largely mirrored what I've heard from poets and novelists. More often than not, songwriters discuss points of entry into creative worlds of uncertainty. They cite familiar triggers: a feeling, an experience of nature, a love relationship, a question, notion, urge, an observation in everyday life. These are points of entry sometimes just for writing lyrics and on occasion for creating both lyrics and melody. But songwriters also seem to have triggers for writing music in ways that are unique to this art form.

Blues musician Paul Reddick, for example, says he often looks to poetry as a point of entry. His songs find a spark in a poem's shape, pattern, and rhyme. He will use either one of his own poems or a published work he happens upon—whatever stimulates his imagination. (He is a collector of books from childhood.) But what is particularly compelling is that the poetry, for him, disrupts traditional musical form and adds interest to what he eventually creates.

"Just the idea of writing in different structures in turn altered the structure of the music," he tells me. "Blues is primarily a twelve-bar form. I often instinctively shy away from writing traditional blues music. It's beautiful, but I want to explore something else. Poetic form actually helps me make changes in song structure that is much more interesting."

Reddick regales me with stories about how he engages with verbal form, vowel sounds, and rhymes. I find myself particularly entertained by his riff on how he rhymed "silhouette" and "cigarette" in one of his tunes and how that affected the outcome. It is charming to learn about his process of discovering music through a playful encounter with words.

Songwriter and singer Alana Bridgewater tells me about a variety of ways in which she begins the writing of songs. As with Reddick, she too will often use her own poetry as a starting point in a manner that ultimately affects the structural shape of the music. But she also says that, as the process evolves, she eventually hears music in her head and feels it in her body. "As soon as the poem begins to convert into song lyrics," she explains, "the music starts to come through. And so then I start moving, you know."

"Moving? Physically?"

"Yeah, moving."

"And that melody," I ask, "how does it evolve?"

"I hear it internally. And then I will sing it and eventually record it."

Kurt Swinghammer doesn't use poetry or a formal play with language to enter his songwriting, but he speaks about playing with rhythm and time signatures that function similarly. "I have certain goals when I'm writing a song. One of them is not to repeat what I've done before, not relying on traditional chord structures that I've done or have heard a million times. One thing I try to do is to write in asymmetrical time sequences, like fives and sevens and nines and elevens, instead of fours and threes, which is 99.9 percent of the music we hear in our culture."

"And what do those rhythms end up doing for you in your process?"

"They produce something just different enough to excite my ear. And then I try to find chord combinations that follow and that I've also never heard."

Dave Bidini talks about a process of using unfamiliar chords as his stimulus for songwriting. His use of the "strange sound" as an entry point into the writing is his version of what these other songwriters have said. "Our drummer once said to me (and so did David Crosby and Joni Mitchell, by the way), 'If you are looking to write a new song, try to use a chord you've never used before.' That was the case, for example, with the song 'Horses,' which is on our second album. In that instance, it would have been a B7th diminished—oh no, actually it was an A7th diminished! And I played it in the second position on the neck—not the first—so it was also in a little bit of a different place on the neck too."

Amused, as we both are, at his initially misremembering the actual chord that sparked him, I ask, "And that was your point of entry into writing that song?"

"It was! As soon as I struck that chord, it just opened new possibilities, all because the chord was unfamiliar to me. That was the way into it. I found the chord and then I built a chord sequence [a frame]. And then I had a conversation with myself: 'Is it going to be fast? Is it going to be slow? Is it going to be this, is it going to be that?'"

There are times, however, when an artist is not aware of any trigger at all as the writing of a song begins. In fact, the sudden recognition of a tune "in the head" will often lead to the sensation for a musician of a melody spontaneously arising from within. Songwriter and singer Hillel Tigay offers an interesting perspective on this experience. Tigay's life *is* music. He is, in his own words, "passionate and obsessive about it." We have seen the definition of making extend well beyond the moment in the studio, the rehearsal hall, or the act of writing itself. That observation had specific relevance to a single, isolated project. But what if one's life is a continual project of invention? What if, like Tigay, the passion and obsession are so extensive that the artist is in a perpetual mode of making? How wide is the spectrum then?

As I listen to Tigay talk about his experience, I become aware that for this artist (and it's not hard to extend the idea to many of the others I've interviewed) there is no real separation between ordinary life and creative life. When you are as passionate as he is, it all blends into one.

"I am addicted to music, and I love it, and I love beauty, and I get a huge amount of pleasure from the challenge of doing it, even the struggle." Curiously, this is a person seemingly in a persistent mode of creativity. It's almost biological, and I'm therefore not surprised when he compares his work to having a child. "I can't describe the feeling to someone who hasn't done it, what it feels like to have an idea and wrestle with it. It's like being a parent. You create something, because you have some urge to do it. It gives you great pleasure, and you hold the outcome as your own. A great piece of music that I put out, and that I feel is high quality, is like a beautiful child to me. And each time I do it, it happens anew, and it's another child."

For Tigay, making comes from a deep connection with music and what it yields. At times, it can unite him with something otherworldly, something sublime. "I've always been connected to music. People don't listen to poetry in the way they listen to music. Music is abstract and moving. And there's something divine about things that are abstract and moving. It allows us to tap into something unknowable, like God, I suppose. The trigger for me is always the melody, and its texture. It's something abstract that can't be influenced by something literal."

Tigay tells me that melodies are coming to him all the time. His point of entry is nothing but a readiness to respond. "It's just about being in an emotional state where doors suddenly open and something comes out. I've written songs in my dreams—and those can be great because I'm not getting in the way of it. Most of the time we get in the way of ourselves."

"Can you tell me in more detail what actually happens creatively?"

"I access some little piece of my subconscious. There is a lot of beautiful art in everybody's brain. The key is figuring out how to access it, and then knock it down when you see it. For me, I try to capture the stuff that is circulating in my head. But it comes to me in different places, and not necessarily when I'm at the instrument. Sometimes, I will be in the shower or exercising or swimming or walking—or dreaming. There's some motif in my head. And I will pull out a recording device and sing it."

"You hear the melodies internally first?"

"I often do, and sometimes even with a lyric. But usually it's just the melody. And then at some later point I will fill the melody with lyrics or I will add a bridge or a verse. But not until I have improvised and worked with the song. There's the inspiration and then there's improvising. There's no way not to improvise."

IMPROVISING IN SONGWRITING

Poetry, unfamiliar chord sounds, strange time signatures, a disciplined and persistent readiness—these are some of the entry points into writing songs for these artists. What happens next, as Tigay makes clear, is often improvisational ("always" improvisational for Tigay), in a variety of forms and through several techniques. The stories these artists tell about the creation of their songs, how they work to propel their making, are deeply compelling.

Tigay, as we have just seen, transitions from hearing a melody internally to the improvisational part of his work. "I just sit down at the instrument and I play and play. Just improvise. Frankly, ninety percent of it is complete shit. I regularly feel like quitting and always think that I suck. But then, once in a while, it's like 'Oh, what did I just do? That was actually kind of good.' It seems I can go from feeling like quitting to suddenly coming across a good idea and sitting there for ten hours in a row, playing it over and over again. I will obsess about it. If it's good, I can keep working to make it better. I'm improvising to build it, to create a bridge, to structure it, to fill gaps with lyrics, and then to create the arrangement."

"And so what begins as music in your head, then actually goes through a fairly radical process of change?"

"It's in my head, but I can't think in five dimensions at once. My brain can hold the melody, which is a simple thing to do without an instrument. And I can even have a lyric and chord progressions in my mind. I can feel the mood and the texture of the song. But there will always be steps that happen later, when I'm improvising. Is it better on the piano? Or maybe better on guitar? What rhythm should I use for the verse? What about the chorus? Improvisation is essential to getting at it all. I can think three-dimensionally but not five-dimensionally. I cannot think of it all."

"Say more about what improvisation is for you."

"The word 'improvisation' is probably misused in music because of jazz. People assume improv is when you go on a flight of fancy with the main melody. But I'm talking about how the song is made. Everything other than the initial quick inspiration is improvisation. I'll loop something on the computer and then I'll just improvise on top of that."

Tigay improvises on his own most of the time. Sometimes he brings in singers and other musicians to experiment with elements of the song, but mostly he is using his instruments and various technological devices to create his music.

Swinghammer, similarly, after experimenting with unusual rhythms and time signatures, improvises on his own to shape and ultimately to find a song. "It's about trying things. What happens if I put this note next to that? How should I sequence things?" He then talks about failure and how he learns from that. "Sometimes it's just wrong. I need to try something else. But the mistake I would normally try to avoid actually gives me something to respond to. That's what improvisation can do—and it helps make sense of it all. And when I do find something, I then have to record it. Otherwise it goes into the ether."

There are other forms of improvising that take place not on one's own but in collaboration with fellow musicians. Alana Bridgewater will sometimes go from a point of inspiration—hearing the music internally and feeling it in her body—to working with a piano player to improvise the development of the song. "After I record it the first time, in a basic way, I will see my piano player, and we will expand it. We just start riffing. It's writing on the fly. I just start singing. We don't know what will come out."

175

What Bridgewater goes on to explain about her experience of improvising and "riffing" is that it leads to hearing "internally" other parts of
the music not heard before. "As I'm working out the rudiments of music
and the song begins to take shape through improvisation, I begin to hear
other elements, like percussion and the bass and the full instrumentation. Even if the song is not complete, even if I'm working just with the
guitar, I can already hear the piano, and the drums, and I hear the bass."
Her process moves between hearing the music and improvising it to its
next level of realization.

Paul Reddick's process of developing lyrics for the tunes he creates that
are still in an early, rudimentary state (tunes that are themselves influenced
by poetic form) involves dictation. "I voice text all the time, because the
way I speak is different from the way I write. With speaking, I'm free from a
certain artifice of writing. Dictating brings out something I'm feeling intui-
tively, or what I'm thinking about, and it's like some sort of subconscious
release." For this artist, the spontaneously spoken word yields a different
quality and feel to his work. It's more honest. As we saw with his use of
poetry, Reddick is inspired by form and texture. "I play with the tone of the
word, and then I try to make it so that when I sing those words they feel
good coming out. Every word has a different dynamic quality and that's
how I know the song. I don't sing the songs from an emotional base. I sing
them more as a roller coaster across the words melodically."

"And the music? Can we go back to that? How does it evolve? Is it
improvised as well?"

"I sing and play harmonica. I don't play the guitar or piano. So
I'll improvise little baselines or snippets of music and record them
on my phone or on a tape recorder. And then I'll go to guitar players
whom I worked with before, who understand what I'm doing, and
they translate it for guitar. And it is, really, a translation. It doesn't
come out exactly as it was in my head. And that's an important part
of the process. It gets altered. And then I will go to the bass player and
the drummer. And it changes more. Each musician has their way of
doing things, adding their understanding of what I am doing with the
song. And I don't try to control the process. What I end up with really
depends on who I hired to explore and to reveal the songs that I write."

Finally, it is instructive to return to Bidini's story of "Horses" and how that song emerged through improvisation in the form of fortuitous association following the spark of the strange chord. As we learned, the unfamiliar chord led him to improvise a new chord progression. But then "happy accidents" took over. First, he became focused on horses by way of a chance encounter with an Alex Colville painting. That in turn led to an association of horses with labor. With that idea on his mind, a media-heavy story of the day (it was the winter of 1986) caught his attention with a particular power. It was the Gainers meatpacking strike in Northern Alberta. Bidini was moved by what he saw and heard about the plight of the workers. The story compelled him to create the song

Alex Colville (1920–2013), *Horse and Train*, 1954. Glazed oil on hardboard. Art Gallery of Hamilton, Ontario, Canada. Gift of Dominion Foundries and Steel, Ltd., © A.C. Fine Art Inc.

Gainers meatpacking strike in Edmonton, Northern Alberta, Canada, 1986.

as an homage to their strike and to the people it affected. It formed the core of the song. "I followed that narrative along, and then built a narrative around a striking worker in that wintertime. That's the anatomy of how that song came together," he says. Improvisation for "Horses" took the form of responsiveness to the fortuitousness of experience.

Improvisation in songwriting can be a collaborative process in the way Reddick describes. Some artists, like Tigay, tend to go through the invention process on their own, either on acoustic instruments or through technological devices that allow them to build and loop multiple sounds. Others, like Reddick and Bridgewater, might construct their songs through a sequential process of collaboration, musician by musician. Still others, like Bidini, ride a wave of unpredictable chance. The melodies may well exist in the heads of their creators and come to them through specific triggers. They might even come to them seemingly involuntarily (especially when the creative sensibility infuses just about everything they do). After an improvisational session, an artist may even hear more internally, as Bridgewater does. Ultimately, except when a song arrives "perfectly," a process of making, of improvising, is necessary to bring it to life. Improvisation is the pathway to knowing the song, reminiscent of artists and designers who "draw through," "write through," or problem-solve their way to discovery.

And yet, there is still another critical step in making that happens with singer-songwriters, a step that is distinctive and vital: performance.

PERFORMANCE

"And then when you perform the song," I ask Alana Bridgewater, "how does it connect with your experience of writing?"

"I'm discovering the song in different ways. It becomes something new to me. Every audience is different. When I'm performing, I discover things. As I am singing, there will be moments of enlightenment. I'll want to move in one direction or another. I'll feel this is too much, or I need to take it back. It changes all the time."

Bridgewater's creative process follows a course from poetry to lyrics to melodies to improvising with fellow musicians. But the differentiating element for her is always live performance. That is the context that requires her to be attentive in a way that will change the song, shape it, find its points of beauty. "When I'm performing, I am discovering things." And each time it is different. Even though not formally an improvisation, live performance by definition is real-time invention, even in minute ways, and thus the making continues through the presentation. As a work of art created expressly for performance, the song's realization is in the singing. And in the next singing. And the next.

As Paul Reddick puts it: "When it's live, it always evolves." But he adds this insight: "I play with different bands and musicians all the time. They have different habits and different understandings of what to do. Through those differences, I'll realize something about the song I've never known. Sometimes it feels right, other times terrible. It's always an adventure."

Dave Bidini initially echoes both Reddick and Bridgewater in his description of performance: "Performance is existing in the moment. You can spend a lot of time in your room, composing your music, and a lot of time in the studio, but you know, live, it's all happening. It's all being kind of born all over again." But then he goes on to describe the continuous discovery of subsequent performances of the same song. "I've always enjoyed the jeopardy of taking songs and playing with them, stretching them, and taking them live to different places. We do it sometimes to amuse and thrill ourselves, occasionally to a fault, but that's fun too. And the audience knows you're walking on that tightrope, and you're trying different things with the song, especially with a known song that has a known form. Creatively, that's really, really thrilling."

Bidini calls out the "jeopardy" of these performances, the risk. Bridgewater, on the other hand, describes it as vulnerability. "At the root of performance is a vulnerability that you have as an artist. I think it's important to be vulnerable. People don't want to see a façade. You have to show your humanity, otherwise you're just a caricature. There has to be vulnerability." And in that vulnerability Bridgewater finds the strength of the song. "It allows the song to speak, the song to move, and the spirit joins it, and then communication happens." And it is only in performance that Bridgewater can bring it all to completion: "I just open myself to what is. I listen to what the message is. I listen to the words. And I sing."

As I pointed out earlier in this chapter, there is a vitality that comes from the risk of live performance, from its jeopardy and its necessary vulnerability. The artist discovers in the moment and extends the creative act. That's what performance yields. We learn about Shakespeare's plays through performance. To study the plays as literature is one thing, but to realize them in performance—their ultimate purpose—brings them to a completely different level of actualization. And each subsequent performance, and each production, realizes something else. That is why audiences still find the plays interesting, even after more than 400 years of production. Songs function similarly. In its composition, a song may come easily to the artist. It may persist like an earworm or take shape through improvisational development. But singing, with an audience present, is the culmination. When it is live, performance is a making of its own.

Chapter 6

IMPLICATIONS FOR HOW WE LIVE

The only way to understand leadership is to lead. The only way to understand marriage is to get married. The only way to understand whether a certain career path is right for you is to actually try it for an extended period. Those who hover on the edge of a commitment, reluctant to make a decision until all the facts are in, will eventually find that life has passed them by. The only way to understand a way of life is to take the risk of living it.
—RABBI LORD JONATHAN SACKS[1]

What I cannot create, I do not understand.
—RICHARD FEYNMAN[2]

We do it all the time. We make to know. It's a way we communicate, learn, understand. In just about every conversation and every interview I have conducted, the discussion about making and knowing extended beyond the specific practice of art and design. Repeatedly, people expressed that make to know is germane to the way they build careers, the way they teach and learn, the way they live their spiritual lives, or even the way they engage in loving relationships with others. Make to know is as everyday as ordinary speech. Creative engagement in worlds of uncertainty is part of living and integral to our development, from the earliest days of childhood onward. Make to know is all around.

Neuroscience provides some intriguing clues to how this central experience of making and knowing works. Researchers have used functional MRI (fMRI) machines to examine the neural substrates that underlie our creative endeavors. Some of the emerging discoveries in this area may help us to understand how the relationship of making and knowing, and the creativity of everyday, shapes the way we live.

Charles Limb of the University of California, San Francisco, is an otolaryngologist known for his work on the neural basis of creativity, particularly as it relates to improvisational jazz. In 2008, together with Allen R. Braun, Limb employed a fMRI machine to explore what happens to the brain during improvisation.[3] Inspired by his own passion for the masterpieces of John Coltrane, he wanted to know what we might learn from the brain activity of an improvising jazz musician. He set up a mechanism that would allow musicians to play on a keyboard while in the machine, observed what the fMRI revealed about their brains in creative mode, and reached a number of important conclusions.[4]

Jonah Lehrer, in his book *Imagine*, summed up two of Limb's findings that are particularly relevant to this discussion. First, the fMRI images of the improvising musician revealed "a surge of activity in the medial prefrontal cortex, an area at the front of the brain that is closely associated with self-expression." And second, "there was a dramatic shift in... the dorsolateral prefrontal cortex (DLPFC)....The DLPFC is most closely associated with impulse control...it's a neural restraint system....Before a single note was played in the improv condition, each of the pianists exhibited a *'deactivation'* of the DLPFC, as the brain instantly silenced the circuit."[5]

The activation of the medial prefrontal cortex, that part of the brain related to daydreaming, personal memories, and expression (Limb, in a TED talk, referred to it as the "center of autobiography"),[6] suggests at minimum that improvisational activity is a peculiar, even idiosyncratic communication, powered by a part of the brain that enables the expression of something uniquely characteristic of the maker. On the other hand, the deactivation of the DLPFC—that part of the brain that can inhibit and serve as a restraint system—is similarly striking for what it liberates. If improvising depends on the brain silencing inhibitions that would be an impediment to a certain kind of expression, then we can understand this kind of making as a means of getting at something that would otherwise be blocked (although sometimes the blocks exist for very good reasons).

The knowing that comes from making is not simply about the thing made. It is also a means, potentially, of self-discovery and self-knowledge, and, as such, it sets up the possibility of a powerful and honest assertion born of that discovery. The activation of that part of the brain specifically associated with "autobiography," together with a release of inhibitions in another part of the brain, connects creative making in an improvisational mode with the way we access (and know) our personal stories. Creativity, understood as neurological activity, is a way toward uncovering something about who we are.

What might Limb's work suggest about the everyday of make to know? Interestingly, his co-author, Allen Braun, has observed that the brains of improvisers mirror the brains of people dreaming in REM sleep. "It's tantalizing to think some connection exists," Braun reflects, "between improvisation and dreaming, which are both spontaneous events. These musicians may in fact be in a waking dream."[7] This suggestion opens up the curious possibility that dreaming, a regular part of our experience, could itself be a make-to-know process, an everyday creative activity that gives potential access to the self.

In a riveting conversation, Jungian psychoanalyst James Hollis speaks to me quite explicitly about dreams as a make-to-know of the soul. "Sleep research tells us that we have on average six dreams per night (or approximately forty-two a week). And nature, apparently, doesn't waste energy. It's obviously doing something important for the system. And part of that can be simply processing the raw material that life hits us with every day. So when people are deprived of dreaming, they can often, after a few days, wind up hallucinating, as if somehow that material has to be processed regardless. But if we begin to pay attention to our dreams, we realize that there is an extraordinary creative process in the human psyche. I am always astonished at that creative power that exists in any of us. The dreams can be elliptical and elusive, of course, but tracking them over time leads one to a greater sense of personal authority and personal grounding in one's own identity."

Neuroscientist Aaron Berkowitz, in his book *The Improvising Mind*, discusses an fMRI study that he conducted in 2008 with his colleague Daniel Ansari.[8] Again, the scientists involved in this work observed the brain activity of various musicians improvising on the piano. One of their most striking findings was the activity they noted in the inferior frontal gyrus, a part of the brain that "is most closely associated with language and the production of speech."[9] Of the many intriguing results of this study, the relationship Berkowitz explored between improvisation and speech is most relevant to the idea of make to know in everyday experience.

Speaking in normal conversation is improvisational by definition; we draw on our reservoirs of language and grammar (the linguistic system) and use that material to speak in the moment to others. We have a context for the conversation (the frame) and even a sense of what we want to say. But the only way to know fully what we wish to express is to speak, *to make* speech. We work things out *while* speaking. We engage in a creative process called speech that brings us to a deeper, more detailed form of awareness about how and what we think. Our knowledge may be partial, but the speaking brings us closer to understanding our thoughts more fully. Making speech helps us know. As Merleau-Ponty wrote in his essay "On the Phenomenology of Language": "My spoken words surprise me myself and teach me my thought."[10]

Linguists Rosamond Mitchell and Florence Myles argue similarly in *Second-Language Learning Theories* that "spoken language is a complex mix of creativity and prefabrication."[11] By looking at language acquisition based on studies of second-language learners, they determine that speech is certainly a creative process, but one that relies on the capacity to access a given linguistic system—something we learn through practice and repetition. As the musician draws on skill and experience to improvise creatively with a system of notes and rhythm, as the writer with words and grammar, as the sculptor with material and form, so too the maker of spoken language leverages acquired skill and experience to engage in a creative endeavor. The principles of make to know are evident in everyday language and speech.

Psychoanalyst Adam Phillips explores in his work how the therapeutic context—and the speaking that takes place within that context—is similarly a make-to-know process of self-access. As he discusses in his lecture "Against Self-Criticism," the very process of free association in analysis is essentially make to know: "We don't know the value of what we think and feel before we say it—it is in the saying of it that we might discover it."[12] There is, certainly, an improvisational element to analysis, and its very process echoes principles of entering uncertainty, improvising within a frame (the space, the relationship with the therapist, the allotted time), and the possibility of finding the surprises and recognition of an embedded creative practice in the psychotherapeutic context.

In an interview with Daphne Merkin at the 92nd Street Y in New York (June 2014), Phillips explored similarities between writing and analysis. He made a simple but powerful statement: "The extraordinary thing about writing is that things *do* occur to you." The same, of course, can be said of speaking in the context of psychoanalysis. Phillips cites Richard Poirier's fascinating work *The Performing Self* and refers to his own writing as "another way of performing myself...I perform myself in language."[13] Again, the performative is, as we discovered in the last chapter, a fluid process, one that can reveal things that might otherwise be inaccessible.

Phillips added a further layer of insight to which I imagine many artists would relate. He reflected that, much like analysis itself, writing for him does not always lead to an *immediate* knowing. On occasion, he doesn't know what his writing means or fully understand what has come out. It is as elliptical as the dreams James Hollis references. But like Hollis's tracking of dreams over time, Phillips will ponder his elusive writing on the condition that "it doesn't ring false and [it] has a good rhythm to it."[14] Phillips's point is well taken and squares with what we have learned from artists and designers about the creative process: the knowing is not always instantly apparent. It may need time or the unusual prompt of a different context (the shower, the drive, the dishwashing) to understand and develop more fully. To reiterate the central issue, we learn that making is not always direct engagement with the work (or the dream); the making/knowing relationship will extend beyond the studio, the writing, the therapist's office.

THE CREATIVITY OF TRANSITIONAL OBJECTS

Make to know is evident in our earliest stages of development as human beings. Again, psychology offers a noteworthy perspective. In 1959, psychoanalyst Selma Fraiberg wrote in her book *The Magic Years* about how a child in the first eighteen months of life learns mobility—to crawl and to walk. Her work uncovered something important about how we, as human beings, move forward to know things. What she identified about the developing child also anticipates processes in later stages of life when human beings enter spaces of uncertainty and, ultimately, creativity.[15] Indeed, Fraiberg's discussions about the toddler learning to crawl and walk, separating from the parent/caregiver in an anxious act of navigating an unknown world, holds deep resonance for the making/knowing dynamic. She describes how some toddlers, when learning to walk, hold small transitional objects as they make their way—perhaps a strategy to carry something of the parent/caregiver with them, even as they venture into the unknown.

The psychoanalyst most famous for exploration of object relations, Donald Winnicott, talks about the transitional object of the child as something more than the self-soothing instrument we typically assume it to be. The investment in the object, he argues, suggests a first *creative* act of the child, who has taken something (from the parent/caregiver) and has *made* it their own. This act of "making" the transitional object transpires in a new psychic place, what Winnicott calls an "intermediate zone," or "potential space" of transitional phenomena. The language is striking and entirely relevant. The potential space, like the cosmology developed by the maker, is a space of the unknown, a space of fear, but it is also one of discovery. The child holding the object when beginning to walk, entering uncertainty, parallels what happens to the artist when embarking on a creative journey. They both enter places of rich unknowing.

The equivalent "transitional object" for the artist is the scaffolding of experience, skill, education, etc.—all key supportive elements that "become one's own" and embolden first steps into uncertainty. These elements can all function as potential spaces, to use Winnicott's language, and serve as a way into both a sea of anxiety and the possibility of mobility. Winnicott also refers to the potential spaces of transitional phenomena as "epistemological spaces": spaces of *knowing*, in which something new is encountered, discovered, recognized.

A further interesting point is that a transitional object can become a fetish if the child is unable to internalize its soothing, comforting qualities and then leave it behind. The child needs the object, now the fetish of anxiety, to feel safe. In the well-known *Peanuts* cartoon, Linus cannot go into the world without his blanket; he is unable to carry the comfort of that object internally. We hold on to the fetishized parts of our lives precisely because they give us comfort. But by doing so, we stagnate. If we cannot find renewal from the strength born of internalizing what the object represents, then we become reliant on an external crutch.

Is there a parallel for the artist? There are many who express a sense of having sometimes been stuck on the scaffolding. For a time, they lose the capacity of reaching into uncertainty and instead cling to already-mastered skills, personal theories and ideas, past experience, and formal inclinations—all of which, like transitional objects they cannot seem to let go, guarantee them a kind of safety. But there are consequences to this state of affairs. Clutching the familiar, these artists find habitual and repeated gestures in their work, stylistic ruts, and obsessive recurring images. They are trapped. As we saw in a previous chapter, for painters like Tom Knechtel and illustrators like Wendy MacNaughton, the process of making itself—painting through it, drawing those coffee cups over and over again—can be key to getting unstuck, a way of reintegrating creative energy.

Just as the child needs eventually to internalize that which assists in growth and development, so too the artist. To stay creative and in motion, the artist requires the internalized strength to take risks and find new worlds. Without this, the artist is caught and, in the language of psychoanalysis, is a fetishist.

EDUCATION

In addition to its everyday manifestation, make to know is significant to how we might think about education on all levels. To understand this, I extrapolate what I have learned from a career focused on the education of artists and designers. The studio curricula at many of the art and design colleges with which I am familiar follow an applied project-based approach.[16] This is a methodology that shares some of the fundamental elements of make to know—entering uncertainty, engaging material, problem-solving, and improvisational exploration. The overarching educational philosophy of these schools is one that quite deliberately throws students into a deep-end learning experience, through which they need to "make" their way to understanding and knowing.

First, instructors in these colleges typically offer a variety of assignments and projects using as points of entry provocative questions, psychological and sociological quandaries, political challenges, values of diversity, equity, and sustainability, ethical and personal interrogations, or clearly articulated design briefs resembling what students will encounter in their professional careers. These points of entry are all prompts for students to confront the unknown and to discover what that creative space of uncertainty might yield. Parallel to that approach is the teaching of technique. Students develop skills of making through the traditional shop as well as through technologies of rapid prototyping, laser cutting, 3D printing, and the like. They develop expertise in relevant software programs, modeling, finishing techniques. They hone critical thinking skills and find meaning in an expanded study of the humanities and sciences, sensitizing them to issues of human experience that make them better artists and designers. And they learn to draw. They learn to see in a way that only the act of drawing can yield. It is a fundamental practice. All of this forms the scaffolding that allows them to reach with increased confidence and ability into the creative uncertainties of a make-to-know process. The conviction is clear: the greater the skill, the greater the freedom to discover in the making.

The second fundamental element of a professional creative education includes the learning that comes from the artist's engagement with material. Students study material and enter into "dialogue" with those materials that they employ in a given project, learning about capacity and limitation, constraint and possibility. This is true for fine artists in the use of paint and canvas, charcoal and paper, ink and parchment.

Sculptors, in the spirit of Calder, think with material. Installation art-ists, like Hamilton and Arceneaux, engage the material of space and time (among many other materials). Photographers employ light and the materials of image-making. Digital artists and designers work with media of all kinds. Product designers shape their work in material laboratories and wrestle with issues of access, affordability, and sustain-ability through their choices. And so on. To learn through materiality is to discover the great beauty of the making/knowing relationship and to experience the wonders of material surprise.

The third attribute centers around solving problems as a creative activity for designers. Working through this process of problem-solving, a making popularly termed "design thinking" weaves iterative questions and ideas and an empathetic study of users, with research and prototyping, into a new chronology of discovery. Design thinking, at its best, upends the traditional sequence of "research before making" and instead utilizes research as part of the making, manifesting at all stages of the project. It suggests, moreover, that making can isolate and identify problems not originally understood at the outset, problems that the designer needs to address but that would be impossible to know without the applied practice. It is a process, as well, of building constraints through prototypes and models that bring the designer closer to knowing a solution.

The final element is improvisation itself. No matter what their field of study, students must learn the power of the improvisational. In the applied learning environment, students find inspiration in making/doing where the process of creation and the thing created are one. They learn about building frames for improvisational discovery, about finding beauty in the doing, about recognizing what might become available to them through the process of the work. They discover first-hand the significance of skill and technique to optimize the improvisational. They develop and build on ideas as they improvise.

In short, most art and design educational institutions define the readiness of graduates today not in terms of their preparation as visionaries, but as makers.

One of the challenges with which art and design schools wrestle is how to prepare students in a world that is rapidly changing. How do we train them for jobs that, as we often point out, might not even exist today, or that will evolve in unpredictable ways in the future? The typical answer emphasizes the importance of helping students develop a kind of flexibility that will allow them to transfer fundamental skills to whatever job they take on. That is certainly an important principle. But what grounds that principle, what gives it shape, has everything to do with educating them as makers and sensitizing them to the process of knowing through that making. It is one thing to generalize about flexibility; it is quite another to concretize education as making. That is exactly what will give them the nimbleness they will need.

A current challenge in crafting the overall structure of various degree curricula at art and design colleges tests the commitment to an education of making. All involved in the educational process—chairs, faculty, administrators—want students to be as fully prepared as possible. We want them to develop expertise in their respective fields. We want them to have a comfort and fluency with technology. We want to make sure they understand fundamental principles of business and economics as they launch their careers. We want them to be agents of social change. We want to educate them as whole people through our humanities and sciences offerings. We want them to be interdisciplinary. We want them to have experiences internationally. We want them to be collaborators. We want them, most significantly in these times, to find the beauty and strength of living and working in a diverse world that is inclusive. The list goes on.

The problem that emerges when attempting to meet these many demands is that the result manifests in a curriculum of requirements. Ironically, for schools that teach creative people, required courses, if overdone (as they often are in my estimation), represent one of the most *un*creative ways to build an education. And the need for requirements seemingly never ends. There will always be more boxes to check. The reality is that we work with our students for only a limited amount of time. The practicality and costs associated with higher education are constraints that we need to face. Satisfying a list of curricular necessities is not an inspired solution.

There will, certainly, always be a need for specific courses and designated areas of study in any educational program. My call is not to drop requirements altogether. I wonder, however, if it is possible to think about a curriculum not so much as a series of requirements but, given what we have learned about the make-to-know process, as building frames for discovery? The particular studio classes offered at art and design colleges, with their focus on making and applied learning, can serve as our model for the larger degree programs. We need to construct frames of learning to support "happy accidents" and shape an education in which the learner moves more freely in a space of particular interest. Requirements are born of a *vision* of what we want for our students. Perhaps, if we look instead to building frames, we might foster an overall curriculum in which students can *make* their education.

This conversation about make to know in professional art and design education can have implications for how we teach our children. How can the principles of a make-to-know experience inform the K–12 classroom? How do we teach our kids to enter uncertainty, engage with materials, solve problems, improvise, and learn in a curriculum of frames?

Several schools and philosophies of education have explored these matters or have even employed some of the principles in a very direct way. The constructionist movement in education, for example, calls for an applied pedagogy of making. Constructionists even label one of their teaching methods "problem-based learning." The connections with design thinking are many and fascinating. John Dewey, as discussed in Chapter 1, offered in his philosophy of pragmatism the concept of "learning by doing," an approach that is linked in a profound way to one of the most famous stories of creative education in the West: the Bauhaus movement. Walter Gropius, in his radical work in arts education at the Bauhaus, adopted Dewey's progressive educational doctrines as a fundamental tenet of his pedagogical model.

I have talked with a number of contemporary educators who weave principles of make to know into K–12 education. The work of Professor Doreen Nelson, for example, and her system of Design-Based Learning (DBL), powerfully illustrates how these principles can operate at earlier levels of education. Nelson's emphasis, at least in part, is on what a child might be able to integrate and understand through the three-dimensional creation of a concept, principle, or idea. I have seen in action, for example, teachers using DBL to teach Nathaniel Hawthorne's novel *The Scarlet Letter*. Students built models ("cities") that spatially manifested perceptions of relationship, class distinction, and divisions—or the isolation of Hester Prynne. The students probed deeply beyond the reading as they constructed this three-dimensional structure; they "made" concepts of legalism, sin, and guilt. As Nelson makes clear, these models "were not an end in themselves, but a way to have students think of themselves as the inventors of what they were going to learn—to connect subject matter and creative thinking." And she achieves that goal by turning them into makers. Once the students had created their various three-dimensional worlds, Nelson "taught them to describe their design solutions orally in a variety of settings (one-on-one, small groups, and to the entire class) to own what they had made. My students grew attached to their creations."

In the end, DBL is all about creating a vehicle for students to connect abstract academic concepts to concrete ideas, and to imagine creative solutions to challenges that they confront along the way. It provides a context for students to "perform" their thinking and discoveries. Ideas that they learn in one application may well turn out to serve another field or situation equally well. Hence the learning becomes integrated in an important way and, as opposed to a building of requirements, can serve as a frame of curricular design.[17]

Gail Baker is an educational innovator and teacher-trainer whose commitment to what she calls an "arts-based curriculum" echoes many principles of make to know and dovetails in several interesting ways with the work of Nelson. Baker sees the richness in using the arts as an entry point for learning and discovery, in any area of study. She built an apparatus in the school she founded of critical engagement through music, dramatized stories, performed writing, and improvisation. She set up forms of "making," in other words, that allow students to "know" in a deeper way what they study. "For many children," she tells me, "it was the ticket to understanding or to building understanding on another level." Like Nelson, Baker also believes that the arts allow for an integration not possible otherwise. "The problem with traditional education is that everything is taught in isolation. You learn grammar, you learn phonics, you learn math, and kids become horrible spellers and horrible at math often because they can't make connections. The arts integrate everything."

The work of both Nelson and Baker offers examples of how make to know can begin to change the way we think about education on the K–12 level and addresses the larger question of how we might leverage the relationship of making and knowing to inform education on all levels. If, in fact, one of the fundamental ways of human learning connects directly with a process of making, how does that get translated into an educational program? I believe the implications of make to know for how we educate are vast.

LEADERSHIP

Several years ago, I came across a remarkable story about a design solution for a problematic traffic intersection in the town of Drachten in the Netherlands. It struck me as a story rich in metaphorical significance, especially when it comes to thinking about leadership in a make-to-know context.

At that time (2003), more than twenty thousand cars a day, as well as thousands of bicyclists and pedestrians, would pass through this junction. Collisions were frequent, pedestrians were often injured, and bicyclists were regularly involved in life-threatening accidents. Traffic engineers responded by adding signs and signals that warned motorists to slow down, to be aware of cyclists and pedestrians, and to pay attention to various hazards of the intersection. But despite the added signs and instructions, the dangers persisted.[18]

Enter Hans Monderman, a "counterintuitive" traffic engineer and designer "who hates traffic signs." Monderman brought a very different perspective to addressing the problem. Apparently, he took his cue at least partially from observing people in crowded skating rinks. He noticed that even without any written rules, skaters seemed to avoid each other or slow down and veer in natural patterns to prevent collision. It was similar in some ways to the behavior of a flock of birds or a school of fish, groups that seem to have an instinct for moving together in precise choreography without accident. In Monderman's words, "the trouble with traffic engineers is that when there's a problem with the road, they always try to add something. To my mind, it's much better to remove things."[19] And that is exactly what he did.

Monderman eliminated all traffic lights, warning signs, pedestrian markings, etc., and created instead a roundabout. "There are no lane markers or curbs separating street and sidewalk, so it's unclear exactly where the car zone ends and the pedestrian zone begins. To an approaching driver, the intersection is utterly ambiguous—and that's the point."[20] Through the structure created and the design itself, people naturally slowed down and looked out for each other, and the number of accidents plummeted almost immediately. Why? Because people were more attentive to what they were doing. Because the context brought out something of the best in them—a natural inclination that was missing when rules and regulations dominated. "Pedestrians and cyclists used to avoid this place," Monderman observed, "but now...the cars look out for the cyclists, the cyclists look out for the pedestrians, and everyone looks out for each other. You can't expect traffic signs and street markings to encourage that sort of behavior. You have to build it into the design of the road."[21]

Monderman's traffic solution is not only a powerful example of how design can make a profound difference to human experience, but also a potent metaphor of leadership that employs fundamental principles of make to know. It comes down to a question about how authority functions, a way of thinking less concerned with a top-down vision of how things need to be—with all corresponding rules and regulations—and more about creating a space in which humans can thrive. It is an approach concerned with mining what is inherently caring in people. In the language of make to know, the roundabout is a frame for improvisation. It is a structure that calls upon human engagement in a creative way, a configuration in which people find safety *as they make it*.

A "follow the leader" construct often relies on a model of authority that assumes a vision for what is "right." It presents a path that people must follow in order to realize that vision. By contrast, leadership understood in terms of frames and creating structures for creative engagement is a model that reveals direction through communal making. The principles of make to know in this regard compel us to think about how our leaders might build "roundabouts" for the people they lead. It feels risky, to be sure, to go the route of replacing authoritative vision with what is essentially a journey into uncertainty (like the roundabout itself). Fear of some kind of catastrophe feels like a good reason to cling to individuals who tell us what is right, or who seem able to provide signs for our safety. But Monderman demonstrates that there exists the possibility of greater welfare (and safety) when leaders involve people in the solution.

As Adam Phillips points out in his reflections on Monderman's work: "When the traffic lights were removed—and this is one of at least two familiar kinds of modern story—the assumed catastrophe did not occur. In fact, as luck—or something else—would have it, things were even better than before. There were fewer accidents, the flow improved, there was less rage, more common sense. The other familiar modern story is that the red lights are removed and the consequences are beyond our worst imaginings; this is what tragedies and all political tyrannies are there to tell us about."[22]

In other words, our "worst imaginings" are part of the reason why tyrants can thrive as leaders—they set out a vision to mitigate our fear. But at what cost?

What I am suggesting here about leadership is not a recipe for all situations at all times, or a model that is somehow forever superior. What does compel me is how leadership can draw on the inherent creativity of people and the principles of make to know. I am captivated by the idea of producing spaces for deep "making," driven by values, collective wisdom, and what is best in humankind (avoiding those feared collisions and, instead, naturally working in harmony). I also believe that make-to-know leadership can be exceedingly difficult work, as it calls on the accountability and responsibility of all members of a community and often goes against the grain of expectation and projection of a leader with all the answers. It is a form of leadership that ultimately requires a kind of safety that makes creativity possible (with permission to face all the obligatory stops and starts, successes and failures), made that much more problematic when that safety to innovate stems from an idea—like Monderman's roundabout—that feels anything but secure.

In my own experience, I must confess to confusion when people would ask about my "vision" for an organization I was leading. Perhaps I misunderstood the question, but I always felt as if I were being challenged to describe with considerable precision something that had yet to happen. I felt as if I needed to tell people about the angel I saw in the stone. As I have stated, I never operated that way nor felt that to do so would be best for the community. Again, in each instance I held deep values, a passion for education, a profound commitment to human creativity, experience with sound financial principles, organizational structures, a fundamental ethical framework, and a clear sense of priorities. But that was the scaffolding. The path on which I embarked was one I developed with the community, as together we reached into places of uncertainty. My work was about process, conversation, setting forth and distilling the thoughts and ideas emerging from the creative engagement of a group of students, faculty, staff, trustees, alumni, and community supporters. I saw my work (and still see it) as building a "roundabout" that would set free the inherent wisdom of the collective to determine what a college could and should be. That approach, in my experience, has been one that has produced the finest results with a community that understands its own direction because it has made it, and therefore owns everything about its implementation. It is leadership of make to know.

THE NORTH STAR OF ENTREPRENEURS

In exploring the relationship of principles of make to know with leadership, I reached out to several individuals with experience as entrepreneurs. I was particularly keen on learning the extent to which the entrepreneur took a path to realize a pre-existing vision for a business, as opposed to following a process of make-to-know discovery.

Sam Mann is a successful serial entrepreneur as well as a designer and artist in his own right. When we talk, he tells me several stories about the evolution of his companies and the process of building them.

I ask him: "When you started those companies, did you have a vision for what they would be and the direction they would follow?"

"God no, hell, no," is his response—a fairly typical one among the entrepreneurs I interview. "The thing gets a life of its own, and I was just another cog in the wheel. It's moving. It's the doing of it. For me, it was always the doing of it."

If it is not "vision" that drives the entrepreneur, what is it? Lynda Weinman, dubbed by some "the mother of the internet," offers a most compelling response to this question. In 1995, Weinman joined forces with her husband and business partner, Bruce Heavin, to start Lynda.com. Although it began as a way to further Weinman's work as a teacher and author of a celebrated book on web design, Lynda.com ultimately pioneered a highly regarded and effective approach to online learning. In twenty short years, the company became unparalleled in the size and quality of its online library, and in 2015 LinkedIn purchased Lynda.com for $1.5 billion.

"There was no sort of mastermind vision at the beginning," Weinman tells me. "It was iterative and evolutionary, a process of navigating the different kinds of obstacles and objectives that came along the way."

"But what guided you?" I ask.

"Well, part of it was survival, you know. Sheer pragmatism. It guides you because you have to go where there's a natural need and where you get the validation, the market validation. The other part was a value system, a belief in a way of learning and teaching. That was the North Star."

Weinman goes on to talk about her deep commitment as a teacher. She speaks about rejecting a "mentality of teacher knows best," which to her is anathema to good education. "There is no right and wrong way to learn something. People are different and they need different things. I mean, these labels that we form in our minds (and that were given in school), what we are good at and what we are bad at, needs to be stripped away. That was a big part of my personal value system and my teaching ethos."

Pragmatism and a deep belief in how people learn. Those were the elements of the North Star. They were the guidelines, the scaffolding, the fundamentals. And her point of entry into this journey of uncertainty?

That would be a question of how to democratize technology, how to make it accessible, how to remove impediments to learning in an intimidating high-tech world. "It was a very different philosophy that I think resonated with people," she reflects. "It was more inclusive, nurturing, forgiving, and permissive. My North Star was an approach and a pedagogy, a belief in how people learn and how to treat with respect those who don't know yet. That North Star never really changed."

I think the distinction that Weinman offers between "a preconceived vision" and a "North Star of values" is important to this question of a leadership informed by the principles of make to know. She and Heavin are quite clear that Lynda.com evolved through making, through experimentation, improvisation, and, as Heavin is quick to add, "a lot of failure." The strength of the company emerged through a journey of discovery, and their leadership had everything to do with creating a context in which that could develop.

I conclude my conversation with Weinman by observing how often entrepreneurs are dubbed great visionaries in our culture and how they are often cast, like artists, as people who manifest what they already seem to know.

"It's absolutely the same thing," she responds. "I totally agree with the comparison."

"But maybe they are makers."

"Yeah, I definitely see that. It was definitely true for me."

ENTERING UNCERTAINTY

Above all, remember that you must build your
life as if it were a work of art.
—RABBI ABRAHAM JOSHUA HESCHEL[23]

Finally, I believe the most compelling way to explore the implications of make to know in our lives is to return to the fundamental principle of entering uncertainty. In most aspects of our experience, we face unknown territory: we stand at the threshold of things mysterious, imperceptible, and unfamiliar. And, as we do, we naturally feel fear and anxiety, calculating the risk and danger of entering a place that is strange and confusing. The challenge is all around us, and it can be paralyzing. It is an experience relevant to elements of our lives both large and small, from a decision about how to go about our day to the deepest of spiritual quests.

If artists and designers and their practice of make to know can teach us anything, it is that uncertainty is a space of creative engagement. It is the space where discovery happens through a making that is both playful and imaginative. And it can lead us to know the very thing that is impossible to see before we take the leap. It changes the calculus about how we engage with a life in many ways ambiguous and unknown.

Doing and understanding. Entering uncertainty. Engaging the materials of our lives to discover. Improvising our way to knowing. All of these processes suggest that the human capacity for creativity has deep relevance for just about anything we might face.

In the end, I think, we make life. And as we do, we gradually come to know it.

Notes

Preface

1   Giambattista Vico, *De antiquissima Italorum sapientia, ex linguae latinae originibus eruenda* (1710).

2   Vilhelm Ekelund, quoted in Howard Junker (ed.), *The Writer's Notebook* (HarperCollinsWest, 2008), p. 1.

3   Anne-Marie Carrick and Manuel Sosa, "Eight Inc. and Apple Retail Stores," case study, INSEAD Creativity-Business Platform (INSEAD, 2017), p. 6.

4   "Apple Computer Inc.: Flagship Retail Feasibility Report," Eight Inc., San Francisco—Strategic Design Consultants, August 1996.

5   Walter Isaacson's biography of Steve Jobs conveys Jobs's perspective on the evolution of the Apple Store. For other accounts, see Jerry Unseem, "How Apple Became the Best Retailer in America," *CNNMoney*, August 26, 2011; and Carrick and Sosa, "Eight Inc. and Apple Retail Stores."

6   Carrick and Sosa, "Eight Inc. and Apple Retail Stores," p. 8.

7   Unseem, "How Apple Became the Best Retailer."

8   Eventually, of course, they eliminated the posters in some of the newer stores and replaced them with digital displays. According to Kobe, "Now it's more digital screen kinds of things. We did propose that way back when, but we just couldn't justify the cost in those days."

Chapter 1

1   T.S. Eliot, *The Use of Poetry and the Use of Criticism* (Faber and Faber, [1933] 1964), p. 144.

2   Joan Didion, "Why I Write," *New York Times*, December 5, 1976, p. 270. Adapted from a lecture delivered at the University of California at Berkeley.

3   Umberto Eco, *Postscript to The Name of the Rose* (Harcourt, 1984), p. 28.

4   Tim Brown, "Designers—Think Big!" TED talk, July 2009, https://www.ted.com/talks/tim_brown_designers_think_big/ transcript.

5   Bill Watterson, "Some Thoughts on the Real World by One Who Glimpsed It and Fled," Kenyon College commencement address, May 20, 1990.

6   See, for example, Frank Wilson, *The Hand: How Its Use Shapes the Brain, Language, and Human Culture* (Pantheon, 1998); Daniel Pink, *A Whole New Mind* (Riverhead Books, 2008); Matthew B. Crawford, *Shop Class as Soulcraft: An Inquiry into the Value of Work* (Penguin, 2009); Mihály Csíkszentmihályi, *Flow: The Psychology of Optimal Experience* (Harper and Row, 1990) and *Creativity: Flow and the Psychology of Discovery and Invention* (HarperCollins, 1996); Jonah Lehrer, *Imagine: How Creativity Works* (Houghton Mifflin Harcourt, 2012); Tim Brown, *Change by Design: How Design Thinking Transforms Organization and Inspires Innovation* (Harper Business, 2009); Peter Rowe, *Design Thinking* (MIT Press, 1987); Roger Martin, *The Opposable Mind* and *The Design of Business* (Harvard

Business Press, 2009).

7   For a different take on the issue, especially regarding material engagement, see Pamela H. Smith, Amy R.W. Meyers, and Harold Jo Cook (eds.), *Ways of Making and Knowing: The Material Culture of Empirical Knowledge* (University of Michigan Press, 2014).

8   Darrin McMahon, *Divine Fury: A History of Genius* (Basic Books, 2013), p. xvii.

9   Marjorie Garber, "Our Genius Problem," *The Atlantic*, December 2002, https://www.theatlantic.com/magazine/archive/2002/12/our-genius-problem/308435/.

10 Garber, "Our Genius Problem."

11 Elizabeth Gilbert, "Your Elusive Creative Genius," TED talk, February 2009, https://www.ted.com/talks/elizabeth_gilbert_on_genius?language=en.

12 Immanuel Kant, "Fine Art Is the Art of Genius," *Critique of Judgment* (1790), trans. James Creed Meredith, section 46.

13 Christine Battersby, *Gender and Genius: Towards a Feminist Aesthetics* (Indiana University Press, 1989).

14 Janice Kaplan, *The Genius of Women: From Overlooked to Changing the World* (Penguin, 2020); Craig Wright, *The Hidden Habits of Genius: Beyond Talent, IQ, and Grit—Unlocking the Secrets of Greatness* (HarperCollins, 2020).

15 Harold Bloom, *Genius: A Mosaic of 100 Exemplary Creative Minds* (Warner Books, 2002).

16 David Shenk, *The Genius in All of Us: Why Everything You've Been Told About Genetics, Talent, and IQ Is Wrong* (Doubleday, 2010).

17 Quoted in Garber, "Our Genius Problem."

18 Aristotle, att. by Seneca in *Moral Essays*, "De Tranquillitate Animi" (On Tranquility of Mind), sct. 17, subsct. 10.

19 Margot Wittkower and Rudolf Wittkower, *Born Under Saturn: The Character and Conduct of Artists* (Norton, 1969; reprinted NYRB Classics, 2006), p. 72.

20 Victor Hugo, "A Medley of Philosophy and Literature," *The New England Magazine* (September 1835).

21 Homer, *The Odyssey*, trans. Robert Fagles (Penguin, 1996), p. 77. A more recent translation by Emily Wilson (W.W. Norton & Company, 2017) reads, "Tell me about a complicated man" (p. 105).

22 Isabel Allende in Meredith Maran (ed.), *Why We Write : 20 Acclaimed Authors on How and Why They Do What They Do* (Plume, 2013), p. 6.

23 From Ursula K. Le Guin, "Where Do You Get Your Ideas From?" [1987], in Le Guin, *Dancing at the Edge of the World: Thoughts on Words, Women, Places* (Grove Atlantic, 2017), pp. 192–200.

24 Lorne M. Buchman, *Still in Movement: Shakespeare on Screen* (Oxford University Press, 1991).

Chapter 2

1   Philip Roth in conversation with Terry Gross on *Fresh Air*, National Public Radio (2006). Transcribed at https://www.npr.org/2018/05/25/614398904/fresh-air-remembers-novelist-philip-roth.

2   W.H. Auden, *The Dyer's Hand* (Faber and Faber, [1962] 2013), p. 67.

3   Quoted in Brassai, *Conversations with Picasso* (University of Chicago Press, 2002), p. 66.

4   Nicole Krauss, interview with Rabbi David Wolpe on her fourth

novel, *Forest Dark*, Skirball Cultural Center, Los Angeles, CA, September 24, 2017.

5 John Keats, *The Complete Poetical Works and Letters of John Keats, Cambridge Edition* (Houghton, Mifflin and Company, 1899), p. 277.

6 See Robert Unger, *False Necessity: Anti-Necessitarian Social Theory in the Service of Radical Democracy* (Verso, 2004), pp. 279–80.

7 Charles Baudelaire, "The Painter of Modern Life" (1863).

8 John Dewey, *Art as Experience* (Penguin Perigree, 2005), pp. 33–34.

9 Quoted in *Wilfred Bion: Los Angeles Seminars and Supervision* (Routledge, 2013), p. 136.

10 Richard P. Benton, "Keats and Zen," *Philosophy East and West*, 16(1/2), 1967, pp. 33–47.

11 Donald Schön, *The Reflective Practitioner: How Professionals Think in Action* (Basic Books, 1983), p. 49.

12 Richard Hugo, *The Triggering Town: Lectures and Essays on Poetry and Writing* (W.W. Norton & Co., 1979), pp. 14–15.

13 Amy Tan, "Where Does Creativity Hide?" TED talk, February 2008, https://www.ted.com/talks/amy_tan_where_does_creativity_hide/transcript?language=en. Unless otherwise noted, all subsequent quotes attributed to Tan come from this talk.

14 Tom Stern, *My Vanishing Twin* (Rare Bird Books, 2017).

15 Parker J. Palmer, *On the Brink of Everything* (Berrett-Koehler Publishers, 2018), n.p.

16 Josipovici, Gabriel, *Writing from the Body* (Princeton, NJ: Princeton University Press, 1982), p. 79

17 Tan, "Where Does Creativity Hide?"

18 I borrow the term "cosmic theater" from David Rosenberg, who elucidates his idea of biblical narrative in ways that overlap Tan's cosmology. See his work *Educated Man: A Dual Biography of Moses and Jesus* (Counterpoint Press, 2010) and *A Literary Bible: An Original Translation* (Counterpoint Press, 2009).

19 Peter Wollen, *Signs and Meaning in the Cinema* (Indiana University Press, 1972), p. 113.

20 Rob Feld, *Adaptation: The Shooting Script* (Dey Street/William Morrow, 2012), p. 121.

21 Feld, *Adaptation*, p. 118.

22 Feld, *Adaptation*, p. 119.

23 Paul Valéry, "Recollection," in *Collected Works*, vol. 1, trans. David Paul (Princeton University Press, 1972).

24 Susan Bell, *The Artful Edit: On the Practice of Editing Yourself* (W.W. Norton, 2007).

25 Roland Barthes, *The Rustle of Language*, trans. Richard Howard (Hill and Wang, 1986), p. 289.

Chapter 3

1 From *Henry Moore: Sculpture and Drawings*; quoted in Robert Motherwell, "A review of Henry Moore: Sculpture and Drawings," *The New Republic*, October 22, 1945, https://newrepublic.com/article/99274/henry-moore.

2 Philip Glass quoted in Zachary Woolfe, "Remixing Philip Glass," *New York Times Magazine*, October 5, 2012.

3 Dean Young, *The Art of Recklessness: Poetry as Assertive Force and Contradiction* (Graywolf Press, 2010), p. 62.

4 Ann Hamilton, "Making Not

Knowing," in Mary Jane Jacob and Jacquelynn Baas (eds.), *Learning Mind: Experience into Art* (University of California Press, 2009), p. 68.

5   Ann Hamilton in conversation with Krista Tippett, "Making, and the Spaces We Share," *On Being* podcast, November 19, 2015, https://onbeing.org/programs/ann-hamilton-making-and-the-spaces-we-share/.

6   Peter Brook, *The Empty Space* (New York, Touchstone, 1968), p. 7.

7   John Heilpern, *The Conference of the Birds* (Faber and Faber, 1977), p. 4.

8   In May 2017, I saw Brook's production of *Battlefield* at the American Conservatory Theatre, San Francisco. It was a follow-up to his groundbreaking 1985 adaptation of the ancient Indian saga *The Mahabharata*, a production I also had the opportunity to see at the Brooklyn Academy of Music. *Battlefield* distills one segment left out of the 1985 original (and the original was a nine-hour production!). In a conversation at the time of *Battlefield* with Carey Perloff, then the artistic director of ACT, Brook was quite candid about the fact that, all these years later, he still sees the spirit of make to know as fundamental to getting to an "immediate theatre." He stated it simply and beautifully: "One does, one fails, one moves closer to truth, to knowing truth."

9   Curator Adrienne Edwards sums up the project well: "Intended as an homage to vaudevillian Bert Williams—America's first mainstream black entertainer—the final five minutes of the performance were censored for the television audience, causing Vereen's biting commentary on the history of segregation and racist stereotypes in performance to be lost on viewers at home." See https://henryart.org/programs/screening-discussion-until-until-until.

10   Nithikul Nimkulrat, "Hands-on Intellect: Integrating Craft Practice into Design Research," *International Journal of Design*, 6(3): 1–14.

11   "Rosanne Somerson on the Challenges of Design Education," *Disegno*, January 3, 2014, https://www.disegnodaily.com/article/rosanne-somerson-on-the-challenges-of-design-education.

12   Alexa Meade, "Your Body Is My Canvas," TED talk, September 2013, https://www.ted.com/talks/alexa_meade_your_body_is_my_canvas.

13   Chuck Close interviewed in Joe Fig (ed.), *Inside the Painter's Studio* (Princeton Architectural Press, 2009), p. 42.

14   *Chuck Close: A Portrait in Progress* (1997), dir. Marion Cajori.

15   Wisława Szymborska, "I Don't Know," *The New Republic*, December 30, 1996, https://newrepublic.com/article/100368/i-dont-know.

Chapter 4

1   Poul Bitsch Olsen and Lorna Heaton, "Knowing through Design," in Jesper Simonsen et al. (eds.), *Design Research: Synergies from Interdisciplinary Perspectives* (Routledge, 2010), p. 81.

2   James Self, "To Design Is to Understand Uncertainty," September 8, 2012, *IndustrialDesign.Ru*, http://www.industrialdesign.ru/en/news/view_37/.

3 Recent scholarship on design explores ideas about moving beyond ideas of problem-solving. Writers like Anne Burdick articulate the evolution of design as both a self-reflective practice and an act of political and social significance. The designers interviewed for this book, however, all approached their work from a problem-solving perspective, and I limit my discussion to that concern.

4 Norman Wilkinson, *A Brush with Life* (Seeley Service, 1969), p. 79.

5 Saul Steinberg, quoted in Chris Ware, "Saul Steinberg's View of the World," *The New York Review of Books*, May 26, 2017, https://www.nybooks.com/daily/2017/05/26/saul-steinbergs-view-of-the-world/.

6 E.H. Gombrich, as widely paraphrased from *Art and Illusion* (Pantheon, 1960).

7 *Joan Didion: The Center Will Not Hold* (2017), dir. Griffin Dunne.

8 Didion, "Why I Write."

9 Olsen and Heaton, "Knowing through Design," p. 81.

Chapter 5

1 Although widely reproduced and paraphrased, this quote is most often attributed to Fuller, who was the founder of Habitat for Humanity. See https://fullercenter.org/quotes/.

2 David Morley, *The Cambridge Introduction to Creative Writing* (Cambridge University Press, 2007), p. 128.

3 Quoted in Aaron L. Berkowitz, *The Improvising Mind: Cognition and Creativity in the Musical Moment* (Oxford University Press, 2010), p. 11.

4 Notes to Polyphasic Recordings' CCMC reissue project, quoted at https://en.wikipedia.org/wiki/

CCMC_(band).

5 Santalucia compares the work to Michael Frayn's play *Noises Off* (1982), which dramatizes the offstage world of a theater production.

6 Jerzy Grotowski, *Towards a Poor Theatre* (Simon & Schuster, 1968), p. 21.

7 Grotowski, *Towards a Poor Theatre*, p. 17.

8 Grotowski, *Towards a Poor Theatre*, p. 17.

9 Amy Nostbakken and Norah Sadava, "A Note from the Creators," in *Mouthpiece* (Coach House Books, 2017), p. 11.

Chapter 6

1 Rabbi Jonathan Sacks, "Doing and Hearing," https://rabbisacks.org/doing-and-hearing-mishpatim-5776/#_ftnref5.

2 This quote is said to have been written on Feynman's blackboard at the time of his death in 1988. As discussed in Michael Way, "What I cannot create, I do not understand," *Journal of Cell Science* 130 (2017): 2941–42.

3 Charles J. Limb and Allen R. Braun, "Neural Substrates of Spontaneous Musical Performance: An fMRI Study of Jazz Improvisation," *PLoS ONE* 3(2): e1679, https://doi.org/10.1371/journal.pone.0001679.

4 Discussed in Aaron L. Berkowitz, *The Improvising Mind: Cognition and Creativity in the Musical Moment* (Oxford University Press, 2010), pp. 142–43. See also Limb's TED talk, "Your Brain on Improv," as well as Jonah Lehrer's account in Lehrer, *Imagine*, pp. 89–93.

5 Lehrer, *Imagine*, pp. 90–91. Emphasis mine.

6 Charles Limb, "Your Brain on Improv," TED talk, January 2011, https://www.ted.com/talks/charles_limb_your_brain_on_improv.

7 Quoted in Kevin Loria, "Something Weird Happens to Your Brain When You Start Improvising," *Business Insider*, April 8, 2015.

8 See Berkowitz, *The Improvising Mind*, and also Aaron L. Berkowitz and Daniel Ansari, "Generation of Novel Motor Sequences: The Neural Correlates of Musical Improvisation," *NeuroImage*, 41 (2008), pp. 535–43.

9 Lehrer, *Imagine*, p. 92.

10 Maurice Merleau-Ponty, "On the Phenomenology of Language," in *Signs*, trans. Richard C. McCleary (Northwestern University Press, 1964), p. 88.

11 Rosamond Mitchell and Florence Myles, *Second-Language Learning Theories*, 2nd ed. (Routledge, 2013), p. 12.

12 Adam Phillips, "Against Self-Criticism," https://www.lrb.co.uk/the-paper/v37/n05/adam-phillips/against-self-criticism.

13 Phillips, "Against Self-Criticism." The Richard Poirier book Phillips cites is *The Performing Self: Composition and Decomposition in the Languages of Contemporary Life* (Rutgers University Press, 1992).

14 Phillips, "Against Self-Criticism."

15 Selma Fraiberg, *The Magic Years: Understanding and Handling the Problems of Early Childhood* (Simon & Schuster, 1959). My interest in Fraiberg's work was inspired by my conversation with Aimee Bender, who offered an important parallel in our conversation about entering frightening worlds of creativity.

16 I base my comments largely on my own experiences during the last thirty years at a variety of colleges of art and design. I participate actively in AICAD (the Association of Independent Colleges of Art and Design), a group of thirty-nine leading schools in the United States and Canada. Each school is distinct in terms of the disciplines taught and sometimes in methodology, but all, to a greater or lesser extent, draw on the educational principles I outline here.

17 See https://www.dblresources.org/.

18 Michael McNichol, "Roads Gone Wild," *Wired Magazine*, December 2004. See also Adam Phillips, *Unforbidden Pleasures* (Farrar, Straus and Giroux, 2015).

19 McNichol, "Roads Gone Wild."

20 McNichol, "Roads Gone Wild."

21 McNichol, "Roads Gone Wild."

22 Adam Phillips, "Red Light Therapy," *Harper's Magazine*, May 2016, https://harpers.org/archive/2016/05/red-light-therapy/.

23 From a NBC television interview with Heschel shortly before his death (1972), available at https://www.youtube.com/watch?v=FEXK9xcRCho.

Acknowledgements

This book is about what making reveals, and the story of its evolution is a case in point. But without an exceptional group of generous and talented people, the unfolding could not have ensued. I humbly seek to offer my appreciation here.

I begin with the artists and designers interviewed. At its core, *Make to Know* constitutes stories told by creative people about their process of making. I am the weaver of their tales, but the material is theirs, and I am deeply moved by their generosity and honest insight. I was not, however, able to include all experiences of all people interviewed. In addition to the fifty or so individuals that I was able to feature in this book, there are scores of others who gave of their wisdom. They may not be mentioned directly, but they infuse every page, and I thank them with all my heart.

I was fortunate to work with an exceedingly talented team at Thames & Hudson. I extend gratitude to the astute and ever-thoughtful Lucas Dietrich (and to Jessica Helfand for introducing me to Lucas) and to the caring and proficient Evie Tarr. I would like to acknowledge as well the superb work of my copy editor, Camilla Rockwood—what a blessing to have such skillful and caring attention paid to one's writing. I similarly count as an honor working with the gifted Sean Adams, whose design of the book's jacket I adore.

Two colleagues—Mark Breitenberg and Christina Scavuzzo—were both enormously helpful in the earliest days with research, ideation and the development of a conceptual framework. In addition, Mario Ascencio, the peerless and always generous head librarian at ArtCenter, worked his magic many times in support of this project. And then, at a critical moment in the process, my good friend Dan Polisar flew across the world to engage one-on-one in a three-day intensive retreat—just to talk about the book and to set me on my way. I cannot thank him enough.

In 2018, I was able to take a partial summer sabbatical granted by the Board of Trustees of ArtCenter College of Design. That precious time allowed me to clear my schedule to get some of the writing done. I am particularly beholden to my friend and then chair of the board, Robert C. Davidson, Jr., for his support throughout.

I want to recognize the brilliant guests of *Change Lab*, a podcast I host at ArtCenter. The conversations we had were all extremely stirring, and I am filled with appreciation for the opportunity to enter into dialogue with so many deep creative thinkers and makers. They too influenced this book.

I wish to name as well, as a source of inspiration and encouragement, the incomparable Ann Hamilton, an artist of extraordinary quality and a kindred spirit when it comes to understanding the rich relationship between making and knowing. And if it weren't for my friend Steve Oliver, I might never have had the chance to travel to Columbus, Ohio, to visit Ann in her studio—a meaningful experience I shall never forget.

Several individuals assisted in facilitating interviews with various artists and designers. I wish to mention in that vein the help of Aaron Albert, Leslie Valpy, Doreen Nelson, Melissa Balaban and Adam Wergeles. I am particularly thankful to my dear friend, Leah Cherniak, who singlehandedly opened for me what felt like the entire theater world of Toronto. She made possible interviews with some astonishingly talented performers and directors. I wish to recognize as well the distinguished Soulpepper Theatre Company in Toronto for welcoming me and for providing a place to conduct many of those interviews.

The generous readers of the many drafts of the manuscript (some took in the whole, others individual chapters) deserve to be acknowledged for their time and sagacious advice. To all of them— Kit Baron, Leah Cherniak, Jessica Helfand, Karen Hofmann, David McCandless, Parthy McCandless, Annie McGeady, Dan Polisar, Alison Shapiro, Christine Spines, Tom Stern, Richard Tithecott, Steve Vineberg—my heartfelt thanks. I can't imagine what this book would be without their care and insight. And with that special pride that one can feel only as a parent, I include in that list of valuable readers my son, Zachary, whose design expertise, intelligence and sensitivity are all formidable. What a special feeling to have the guidance of one's child.

In a category unto herself is my friend, colleague and ArtCenter partner, Sheila Low. She does everything—and perfectly. She is smart, creative and dedicated and perhaps the most competent human being on the planet. With this book—and with just about everything else—she exceeded all reasonable expectations of support. I am exceptionally grateful.

I hold profound gratitude to my great life mentors—Francis Martineau, James Hollis, Jed Sekoff, and the late Eleanor Prosser—all of whom have cared for my soul and have given me the strength to find my own creative energy and focus.

And then there's the love. My parents, Faygie and Murray Buchman, are, and always have been, my source of strength and the bedrock of every experience. My siblings and their spouses—Ellen Joy, Stephen, Sandy, Gail—and my siblings-in-law—Ben, Susie, Irv and Kathy—encourage me at every turn; their care and support are with me always.

To my spectacular kids, step-kids and grandchildren—Elissa, Zachary, Shoshana, Jeremy, Ari, Beth, Shira, Judah and baby Roman—your love sustains me.

Speaking of love—I conclude with Rochelle. Much of this book was a make-to-know process we shared. She is a first-rate editor, a brilliant reader, a generous thinker and a woman with the kindest heart imaginable. She was an incredible collaborator. In the words of the Bard,
"I can no other answer make but thanks, / And thanks, and ever thanks...."

Biographies of Artists and Designers Interviewed

Sean Adams is an internationally recognized designer. He is the Chair of Undergraduate and Graduate Graphic Design programs at ArtCenter College of Design and founder of the online publication Burning Settlers Cabin and The Office of Sean Adams. Adams writes for and serves on the editorial board of Design Observer, is the on-screen author for LinkedIn Learning and the author of several best-selling books. He is the only two-term American Institute of Graphic Arts (AIGA) national president in the organization's history. In 2014, Adams was awarded the AIGA Medal, the highest honor in the profession.

Edgar Arceneaux is an artist working in various media including drawing, sculpture, performance, and film. He is an associate professor of art at USC's Roski School of Art and Design. His artwork has been exhibited internationally at the Shanghai Biennale; the Whitney Biennial, New York; the San Francisco Museum of Modern Art; the Witte de With Museum, Rotterdam; and the Museum of Modern Art, New York. Arceneaux is a cofounder of the Watts House Project, a nonprofit neighborhood redevelopment initiative in the Watts neighborhood of Los Angeles.

Gail Baker is a teacher, writer, administrator, and workshop leader. She cofounded the Toronto Heschel School, an arts-based Jewish day school, and served as its head for over a decade. She also cofounded The Intergenerational Classroom, a program that creates integrated learning opportunities for students and seniors. She writes a column for the Lola Stein Institute Journal called "Good Books."

Stephen Beal is an artist, educator, and academic leader. He is president of the California College of the Arts and a professor of painting and drawing. In addition to his academic career, Beal is a practicing artist whose work has been exhibited in the Bay Area and nationally.

Yves Béhar is a designer, entrepreneur and founder and CEO of fuseproject. For Béhar, integrated product, brand and experience design are the cornerstones of any business. He has pioneered design as a force for positive social and environmental change and is at the forefront of entrepreneurial venture design, co-founding FORME Life, August, and Canopy. Béhar has partnered with numerous start-ups such as the Happiest Baby Snoo, Uber, Cobalt, Desktop Metal and Sweetgreen.

Other notable collaborations include Herman Miller, Movado, Samsung, Puma, Issey Miyake, Prada, SodaStream, Nivea and The Ocean Cleanup, many of which have received international acclaim.

Fridolin Beisert is a designer and author. He is the creative director of Baum-Kuchen.net and the director of the product design department at ArtCenter College of Design, where he teaches creative problem-solving, design innovation, and dynamic sketching. Beisert's most recent book is *Creative Strategies: 10 Approaches to Solving Design Problems*.

Aimee Bender is an author and professor of creative writing at the University of Southern California. Her books include *The Girl in the Flammable Skirt*, a *New York Times* Notable Book; *An Invisible Sign of My Own*, a *Los Angeles Times* pick of the year; *The Particular Sadness of Lemon Cake*, winner of the SCIBA award for best fiction as well as an Alex Award; and, most recently, *The Butterfly Lampshade*. Bender's short fiction has appeared in journals such as *Granta, GQ, Harper's, Tin House, McSweeney's,* and *The Paris Review*.

Dave Bidini is an author, musician, and documentary filmmaker. He is a founding member of the Canadian indie rock band Rheostatics. He has written twelve books, including *On a Cold Road, Tropic of Hockey, Around the World in 57 ½ Gigs*, and *Home and Away*. Bidini is the only person to have been nominated for all three of

Canada's main entertainment awards: a Gemini award in television, Genie award in film, and Juno award in music.

Alana Bridgewater is an actor and singer. She was a member of the Canadian Children's Opera Chorus and the Toronto Mendelssohn Youth Choir, and a founding member of the Nathaniel Dett Chorale. In 2007, Bridgewater received a nomination for a Gemini Award for her contribution to the Gospel Christmas Project (CBC).

Anne Burdick is a designer, author, and former chair of the graduate Media Design Practices (MDP) department at ArtCenter College of Design. An area of focus in her scholarly work is defining the future of graduate-level education and research in design. Burdick is coauthor and designer of the publication *Digital_Humanities*. She received the Leipzig Book Fair Prize for the "Most Beautiful Book in the World" for her design of the Austrian Academy of Sciences experimental text-dictionary, *Fackel Wörterbuch: Redensarten*.

Leah Cherniakis a theatre maker, director, actor and teacher. She is cofounder of Toronto based Theatre Columbus (now Common Boots Theatre) and was a Resident Artist with Soulpepper Theatre Company. Cherniak has performed in and directed most of the Common Boots Theatre's repertoire, including the award-winning published play, *The Anger in Ernest and Ernestine*. Most recently, she directed a short film called *Postcards from my Balcony* and co-created and co-directed *Here are the Fragments*, a multi-media immersive theatre piece at Toronto's Theatre Centre.

Joseph Di Prisco is a writer and teacher. He has published several novels (*The Good Family Fitzgerald, Sibella & Sibella, Confessions of Brother Eli, Sun City, All for Now*, and *The Alzhammer*), three books of poetry (*Wit's End, Poems in Which*, and *Sightlines from the Cheap Seats*), two memoirs (*Subway to California* and *The Pope of Brooklyn*) and has co-written two books on childhood and adolescence with the psychologist and educator Michael Riera (*Field Guide to the American Teenager* and *Right from Wrong*). He is the founding chair of the New Literary Project.

Raquel Duffy is an actor and resident artist at Soulpepper Theatre Company (Toronto). A recipient of seven Dora Mavor Moore Award nominations, she won the award for her work in *Alligator Pie*. She also received a Robert Merritt Award for *Mary's Wedding*.

Ann Field is an illustrator and chair of undergraduate illustration at ArtCenter College of Design. Her work has appeared in the *London Evening Standard, Mademoiselle*, and *Vogue Italia*. She has received awards from the Society of Illustrators in New York, *American Illustration, Print*, and *Graphis*. Her work can be found in the permanent collection of the

Cooper Hewitt, Smithsonian Design Museum in New York.

Frank Gehry is an internationally celebrated architect. He is known for designing iconic buildings with complex, curved facades, including the Guggenheim Bilbao, Spain, and the Walt Disney Concert Hall, Los Angeles. He is the recipient of various accolades including the Pritzker Architecture Prize, National Medal of Arts, and Presidential Medal of Freedom.

Nik Hafermaas is a designer and educator. He is managing partner of the Berlin-based innovation agency Graft Brandlab, and the founder of Ueberall International, an artist platform for digital media and spatial experiences. After serving as Chair of Undergraduate and Graduate Graphic Design programs at ArtCenter College of Design, Hafermaas became Executive Director of Berlin programs for the college.

Ann Hamilton is an internationally recognized visual artist known for her large-scale multi-media installations that incorporate videos, objects, and performance. Her work has been shown around the world, including solo exhibitions at the Musée d'Art Contemporain in Lyon, France, and the Museum of Modern Art in New York. In 1999, Hamilton was selected to represent the United States at the Venice Biennale. Her honors include the National Medal of Arts, MacArthur Fellowship, and Guggenheim Fellowship.

Maggie Hendrie is the founding Chair of Interaction Design BS and Chair of Graduate Media Design Practices at ArtCenter College of Design. She also co-directs Data to Discovery, a joint program with Caltech and JPL on interactive data visualization. As an interaction designer and user experience strategist for 25 years, Hendrie has worked across a range of technologies and platforms in both the US and Europe.

James Hollis is a Jungian psychoanalyst in private practice, the former Director of the Jung Society of Washington, D.C., and Director Emeritus of the C.G. Jung Educational Center of Houston. He is the author of 17 books, including *Finding Meaning in the Second Half of Life*; *What Matters Most: Living a More Considered Life* and *Why Good People Do Bad Things: Understanding our Darker Selves.*

Tisha Johnson is Vice President of Global Consumer Design at Whirlpool Corporation. Most recently she served as Vice President of Global Product Design at Herman Miller. Johnson is an automobile designer and the former Vice President for interior design at Volvo. Prior to this, she was the Senior Director of Design at Volvo's Concept and Monitoring Center, where she was responsible for all activities that entailed leading a team of exterior and interior designers in strategic and near-term design proposals.

Tom Knechtel is an artist and former faculty member of the undergraduate fine art department at ArtCenter College of Design. His paintings and drawings have been widely exhibited and can be found in the collections of the Sintra Museum of Modern Art, Portugal; Museum of Modern Art, New York; Museum of Contemporary Art, Los Angeles; and Los Angeles County Museum of Art.

Tim Kobe is an internationally recognized designer. He created the original concept for the Apple Store. He is the founder and CEO of the strategic design firm Eight Inc., which has eight studios across the US, Europe, and Asia. The firm takes a transdisciplinary approach in creating branded experiences that include working in architecture, exhibitions, interior, product and graphic design. Kobe's clients have included Apple, Virgin Atlantic Airways, Citibank, Coach, and Knoll.

Chris Kraus is a writer, art critic, and editor, who navigates the boundaries between autobiography, fiction, philosophy and art criticism. Her work includes the novel *I Love Dick*, recently adapted into a television series on Amazon, *Torpor, Summer of Hate, After Kathy Acker: A Biography* and *Social Practices*. Kraus is coeditor at the influential publishing house Semiotext(e), where she has introduced much of contemporary French theory to an American audience.

Ross LaManna is a screenwriter and author. He is currently chair of ArtCenter College of Design's undergraduate and graduate film departments. He has written original screenplays, adaptations, or rewrites for Fox, Disney, Paramount, Columbia, Universal, HBO Films, and many independent companies. LaManna is best known for writing the *Rush Hour* films, starring Jackie Chan and Chris Tucker.

Michael Laskin is a stage and film actor. He has performed numerous roles off-Broadway and at America's leading regional theaters, including the Guthrie Theater, the Actors Theatre of Louisville, and the Seattle Repertory Theatre. Laskin's film credits include *Just Go With It* (2011), *Eight Men Out* (1988), and *Disclosure* (1994).

Wendy MacNaughton is a #1 *NYT*-Bestselling illustrator and graphic journalist. She has been a visual columnist for *The New York Times* and *California Sunday Magazine*, and is the illustrator of *Salt, Fat, Acid, Heat* by Samin Nosrat, *The Gutsy Girl* by Caroline Paul and the illustrated documentary *Meanwhile in San Francisco: The City in its Own Words*. MacNaughton is the cofounder of the advocacy database Women Who Draw, and creator and host of *Draw Together*, a learning-based drawing show for children.

Michael Maltzan is an architect. He has designed a variety of structures, from private homes to cultural institutions to city infrastructure. His multi-family residential projects have gained international acclaim for their innovation in both design and construction. Maltzan has been recognized with five Progressive Architecture awards and twenty-two citations from the American Institute of Architects.

Samuel J. Mann is an industrial designer, inventor, and entrepreneur. He has more than eighty patents, most notably a quick and sterile system for piercing ears in a retail environment that is now used worldwide.

Courtney E. Martin is an author, speaker, and social and political activist. She is known for her books, including, most recently, *Learning in Public: Lessons for a Racially-Divided America From My Daughter's School*, and her work as a weekly columnist for *On Being*. She also cofounded the Solutions Journalism Network and FRESH Speakers Bureau.

Francis Martineau is a theater practitioner, author, and musician. He has released three solo albums of improvised musical compositions on piano. He has also collaborated and recorded four-hand piano improvisations with David Glass and released three albums with him. He is the author of two novels, *Paddy Whack* and *Venoms and Mangoes*. Martineau was previously a professor at the University of Toronto and, while there, founded the drama program at University College.

Diego Matamoros is an actor. He has performed in theater, film, and television for the past 40 years. In

1998, he co-founded the Soulpepper Theatre Company in Toronto, and in 2006 he established its year-round training program. He has received multiple awards for his performances, both on stage and in film, including a Gemini award for his role as Dr. Goldman in the CBC miniseries *The Sleep Room*.

Rebeca Méndez is an artist, designer and educator. She is a professor and chair in the Design Media Arts department at UCLA and is director of Counterforce Lab, an art and design research and fieldwork studio for projects related to environmental justice. Méndez received the 2012 National Design Award in Communication Design from the Cooper-Hewitt, Smithsonian Design Museum, and the 2017 AIGA Medal for distinction in her field. Méndez's artworks have appeared in a number of institutions including the San Francisco Museum of Art, Hammer Museum in Los Angeles, and Museum of Contemporary Art in Oaxaca, Mexico.

David Mocarski is a designer and chair of ArtCenter College of Design's Graduate and Undergraduate Environmental Design department. He is the principal of Arkkit forms, an interdisciplinary design studio that has created product packaging, furniture design and corporate brand and identity development, as well as residential and contract spatial projects.

Amy Nostbakken is an award-winning director, writer, performer and composer. She is Co-Artistic Director of the theatre company Quote Unquote Collective in Toronto. Amy has co-created and composed numerous productions including *The Big Smoke* (2011) *Ballad Of the Burning Star* (2013), *Bucket List* (2016), *Mouthpiece* (2015) and *Now You See Her* (2018). *Mouthpiece* (Coach House Press & Oberon UK) has been translated into Spanish, French and Turkish and Romanian and was adapted into a feature film directed by Patricia Rozema which opened TIFF 2018. Amy is currently creating QUC's next production *Universal Child Care* set to premiere in 2023. Amy teaches theatre and voice for both adults and young people.

Andy Ogden is a designer and innovation consultant. He is chair of the graduate industrial design program at ArtCenter College of Design. He is also the cocreator and executive director of the Innovation Systems Design (ISD) program, which offers a dual MS in Industrial Design and MBA degree in partnership with the Drucker School of Management at Claremont Graduate College. Ogden was formerly vice president and executive designer for Walt Disney Imagineering R&D and an influential automobile designer for Honda Research of America.

Dennis Phillips is a poet and author. He has written 17 books of poetry, such as *Mappa Mundi* and *Measures* and has translated the work of Italian poets Milli Graffi and Susanna Rabitti. In 1998 he edited and wrote the introduction for a book on the early essays of James Joyce, *Joyce on Ibsen*. His novel *Hope* was published in 2007.

Paul Reddick is a singer, songwriter and harmonica player. He has been performing his critically acclaimed songs on stages across Canada, the USA and Europe for over 30 years. His most recent recording, *Ride the One*, received the 2017 Juno Award for Best Blues Album. Often referred to as the Poet Laureate of the Blues, he has been pushing the boundaries of the blues art form his entire career. His dedication, "Blues is a beautiful landscape", led him to create the annual Cobalt Prize for Contemporary Blues Composition in 2014 which encourages the growth of blues music.

Paolo Santalucia is an actor and director. He is cofounder of the award-winning theatre company, The Howland Company. He is the recipient of two Dora Mavor Moore Awards for Outstanding Ensemble in the Soulpepper Theatre Company (Toronto) productions of *Rosencrantz and Guildenstern Are Dead* and *Of Human Bondage.*

Paula Scher is a noted graphic designer, painter, and art educator. She has created memorable identities and other branding work for clients such as Citibank, Coca-Cola, the Metropolitan Opera, MoMA, the New York Philharmonic, and the Public Theater. Awards include the Art Directors Club Hall of Fame (1998), Chrysler Award

for Innovation in Design (2000), AIGA Medal (2001), and Cooper-Hewitt National Design Award for Communication Design (2013).

Zack Snyder is a film director, film producer, screenwriter, and cinematographer. He is best known for action and science fiction films, such as *300* (2007), *Watchmen* (2009), *Man of Steel* (2013), *Batman v Superman: Dawn of Justice* (2016), *Zack Snyder's Justice League* (2021), and *Army of the Dead* (2021).

Rosanne Somerson is a studio furniture designer/maker, a leader in art and design education, and President Emerita of Rhode Island School of Design (RISD). Somerson also served as RISD's provost and was head of the Furniture Design department, a program that she co-conceived and founded. Her furniture has been exhibited at numerous venues, including the Musée des Arts Décoratifs at the Louvre in Paris, and can be found in the collections of private and public institutions such as the Smithsonian American Art Museum, Yale University Art Gallery, and the Museum of Fine Arts, Boston. She has lectured across the globe and is the recipient of many awards including two NEA Fellowships and the Pell Award for Outstanding Leadership in the Arts.

Tom Stern is the author of the novels *My Vanishing Twin* and *Sutterfeld, You Are Not A Hero.* His words have also appeared in *McSweeney's, Los Angeles Review of Books, Monkeybicycle,*

Memoir Mixtapes, and *Hypertext Magazine*.

Kurt Swinghammer is a singer-songwriter, musician and visual artist. He has released 13 full-length albums of original songs, and as a session musician he appears on over 100 CDs. His artwork is included in the permanent collection of the Canada Council Art Bank. Based in Toronto, Swinghammer has also worked as an illustrator, graphic designer, wardrobe designer, set designer, and art director on music videos.

Diana Thater is a noted artist, curator, writer, and educator. She has been a pioneering creator of film, video, and installation art. Her work is shown in museums around the world and can be found in the collections of the Art Institute of Chicago; Castello di Rivoli, Turin; Los Angeles County Museum of Art; Solomon R. Guggenheim Museum, New York; Whitney Museum of American Art, New York; and the Hamburger Bahnhof – Museum für Gegenwart, Berlin.

Hillel Tigay is a singer, musician and composer. He is the music director and cantor at IKAR in Los Angeles. For his album, *Judeo*, Tigay wrote contemporary melodies for songs with lyrics based on Psalms and traditional Jewish liturgy. He co-founded the former Jewish rap band M.O.T. Tigay released *Judeo Vol II: Alive* in 2020 and is currently releasing an album of contemporary Art Pop music under the moniker Palms Station.

Franz von Holzhausen is an automobile designer. He is currently chief designer at Tesla Inc. and is credited with designing the Model S, Model X, Model 3, second-generation Tesla Roadster, Cybertruck, Semi and Model Y. He previously worked at Volkswagen, General Motors and Mazda.

Esther Pearl Watson is an artist, cartoonist, illustrator, and visual storyteller. Her editorial illustrations have appeared in publications such as the *New York Times*, *McSweeney's*, and the *New Republic*. Her comic strip *Unlovable* has run since 2004 in *Bust* magazine.

Lynda Weinman is an entrepreneur, web and motion graphics designer, and author of multiple bestselling books including the very first publication on web design. Sometimes referred to as the "mother of the internet," Weinman is cofounder and executive chair of lynda.com, a pioneering online education platform established in 1995 and purchased by LinkedIn in 2015 for $1.5 billion.

Picture Credits

Index

/ / | . . now: From Spaces of Uncerta
about creativity. The book upends popular
ad the event of discovery that happens throu
chelangelo, who " saw the angel in the stone, the ar is
ut knowing their work as they engage in the
creative journey itself." As Buchman wea
re learn about writers of all stripes as they
t visual artists and what they understand f
cts and the iterative way process of solving probler
provisational performance. Make to Know is
and, in the end, a stet will have significant im
of Uncertainty to Creative Discovery will
popular notions of innate artistic and visionar italic
" rough the act of making. In con ras to the
one," the artists and designers Buchman i
ae in the doing. Make to Know explores
man weaves together the vivid stories of his r ital
musicians facing the surprises musicians f

Buchman weaves together the vivid stories

ative Discovery will change the way you

nate artistic and visionary genius and probes

f making. In contrast to the classic tale of

ners Buchman interviews for this book tal

ke to Know explores the revelatory nature of

r the vivid stories of his multiple conversati

ive spaces of uncertainty "the blank page"

rials they encounter; about designers and ar

actors and musicians facing the surprises

will, ultimately, open a road to your own ma

for how you live. Make to Know: From Spa

ay you think about creativity. The book uper

robes instead the event of discovery that happ

of Michelangelo, who "saw the angel in 7

is book talk about knowing their work as they

r nature of the creative journey itself. As

sations, we learn about writers of all actors